This book is dedicated to the good people of Barelas . . . and to people everywhere who have struggled for freedom, dignity, and the right of self-determination.

HEART OF AZTLAN

BY

Rudolfo A. Anaya

EDITORIAL JUSTA PUBLICATIONS, INC.
P.O. BOX 9128
BERKELEY, CALIFORNIA 94709

First Printing: December 1976

Copyright © 1976

by   Rudolfo A. Anaya

All rights reserved. No part of this book may be reproduced in any form or by any means without permission in writing, except in the case of brief quotations in critical reviews and articles.

L.C. Catalogue Card Number: 76-55065
ISBN Hardcover: 0-915808-18-8
ISBN Paperback: 0-915808-17-X

CHAPTER ONE

Benjie carefully finished rolling his cigarette, then he leaned back and admired it. Lately he didn't have any money for drugstore cigarettes. He struck the match with his thumb nail and held it to the twisted end of the cigarette. He inhaled deeply. It tasted good. He opened his lips and ringlets of smoke floated lazily towards the ceiling of the outhouse. He couldn't remember the first cigarette he had smoked while sitting on the rough, wooden toilet seat, but he knew this would be his last.

Today they were leaving Guadalupe.

He closed his eyes and listened to the buzzing of the large, black fly that flew around his head. Life in the small town of Guadalupe was like the summer drone of the fly, he thought. it was monotonous; it never changed. He was glad they were leaving. He was fourteen, and already he felt he had done everything there was to do in Guadalupe: play pool at the Eight Ball, drink beer by the lake, fight at the Saturday night dances, and on the last day of school he had taken Consuelo beneath the bridge and scored his first piece. Some consolation, he reflected. She cried and said he had ruined her and now they would have to get married. It scared him. He had seen the other vatos go down the same path, which led to marriage, getting a job pumping gas at one of the stations, and watching your wife get fat year after year. He didn't want that. He wanted to be a part of the excitement and adventure he sensed in the letters his brother Roberto wrote from Albuquerque.

Life beyond the hills that surrounded Guadalupe had always intrigued him. Once they had left the water-enclosed city and traveled east to visit relatives in Tucumcari and he had treasured the strange sights he had seen there. The people were different, and their language and customs seemed different. And of course he had been to Las Vegas in the north, and to the old village of

Las Pasturas in the south, the deserted pueblo whose crumbling adobe walls held so many of the memories of their past. But today they were breaking the confines of the hills and the river valley, and they were moving westward, out of the llano, past the mountains that were but a shadow in the horizon. Tonight they would be in Albuquerque, in a new time and in a new place.

He sang with joy.

"Benjamín! " He heard his mother call him.

Benjie leaned forward and peered through a crack in the weathered boards. He saw his brother Jason standing by the woodpile. He stood like a statue molded from the earth of the llano, silhouetted like a brown Indian against the blue turquoise sky.

. . . *the sky was like a turtle, the old Indian had said, and the sun a white deer that raced it every day.*

Jason's brown chest heaved and glistened with sweat. He was strong, quiet and a year older than Benjie. The women admired his handsomeness. His aunts and his mother's comrades and the women from the town who came to visit all commented on his handsome features; they said he would grow up to be a fine man. Sometimes Benjie felt jealous.

Ah! What the hell, Benjie thought, I'll show them who's the real man in the city. He turned his gaze up the road where a truck raised a cloud of dust. It was don José, the man who was coming to buy their land. In a few minutes their father would sign the paper and the Chávez ranchito at the edge of town would be no more. He took the last drag from his cigarette and dropped it down the hole. He flipped through the worn pages of the Sears Roebuck catalog and tore a few and crumpled them.

Goodbye Guadalupe, he smiled.

"Benjamín! " His mother called again. He walked out of the outhouse, zipping his pants. He looked up at the glaring, white sun. Damn, it was hot already!

"Mamá is calling," Jason said. Sometimes they spoke in Spanish, which was the language of their people, and sometimes they spoke in English, which was the tongue they adopted in school; and so they moved in and out of the reality which was the essence of each language.

"Yeah, I heard," Benjie answered. He walked to the woodpile

2

and looked at the neat stack Jason had chopped. "Why did you waste your time chopping wood, Jason, you know we ain't ever going to use it——"

Jason shrugged. "Somebody will come along and use it," he answered. Benjie shook his head. It was one of those things Jason learned from the Indian, he thought. "Come on," Jason smiled at his perplexed brother, "I think mamá wants us to be with papá. It won't be easy for him to leave his land." He put on his shirt and together they walked around the side of the house where their father stood talking to don José.

"It's the best price I can give you for your ranchito, Clemente, I swear by God Almighty, it's the best offer I can make! " Don José trembled and wiped his sweating face.

"There is no justice in dealing in land," Clemente shook his head. "You offer me Judas money for my three acres, for a home I built from this very earth with my bare hands, for a well blasted a foot at a time out of the hard earth so that I might have water for the jardín and the animals—— You offer me nothing, just enough to pay off my debts, then there is nothing left. When I sell my land I will be cast adrift, there will be no place left to return to, no home to come back to——" He felt the words choking in his throat. He turned and looked at his wife for support and she nodded for him to sign. She understood there was no turning back. He took the contract from don José. His soul and his heart were in the earth, and he knew that when he signed he would be cutting the strings of that attachment. It was like setting adrift on an unknown, uncharted ocean. He tried to understand the necessity of selling the land, to understand that the move would provide his children a new future in a new place, but that did not lessen the pain he felt as the roots of his soul pulled away and severed themselves from the earth which had nurtured his life.

He felt like cursing and crying out the pain he felt. ¡Hijo de la chingada, he cried inside, pero cómo me duele el corazón!

He looked at his sons and knew there would be nothing left to pass on to them. Without the land the relationship a man created with the earth would be lost, old customs and traditions would fall by the wayside, and they would be like wandering gypsies without a homeland where they might anchor their spirit. But he had to go because there was no work in Guadalupe, and because he had to

3

be the leader in helping to create a new future for his familia. He was not the first to leave, many of his vecinos and compadres had already left to make a new life in the bigger cities of Las Vegas, Santa Fe, Albuquerque, and many had gone as far west as California. The people were dispersed, but as they left each one secretly vowed to return to the sacred land of his birth and heritage.

La sagrada tierra . . .

Clemente clenched his teeth and swore, "I will come back, someday——"

Don José chuckled. "They all say that, Clemente, but they don't return. I bought Baca's rancho by the river and he moved to Santa Fe and drank himself to death, I hear, and his sons became marijuanos and they're all in the pinta now. And I bought Luna's place and they say he moved his familia to California, but no one has heard from him since. It is as if the cities swallow them up. But I will tell you what really happens, Clemente. They find work in the cities, and if they are lucky they buy a home, and then they begin to change. Yes, they change and they forget the land," he scowled. "Oh, sure, they talk a lot about returning, but they never do, because they have forgotten. You will see, Clemente, you will forget too——"

" ¡Desgraciado! " Clemente cursed. He snatched the pen and signed the contract. "There," he pushed the paper at don José, "it is done, but if you think the earth can be transferred on a piece of paper then you are crazy! It will abide long after this piece of paper is dust, and my love and memory of it will also survive. How can I forget," he shook his head and pointed south to the llano of Las Pasturas, "my parents are buried in this holy ground," he whispered.

"Dios los bendiga." He heard his wife's blessing.

He crossed his forehead and added softly, "And my brother Guillermo sleeps beneath the grass of the llano—— murdered by that pinche tejano who couldn't keep his wife home! And," he whispered even more softly, "my son, my flesh and blood, rests in the campo santo at Las Pasturas——"

He could not talk anymore; he was afraid his voice would quiver.

" ¡Adelita! " He called his wife and she stepped forward and signed.

"It is done," she said boldly.

Don José surveyed the signatures. "Clemente y Adelita Chávez," he read their names aloud. "Sí," he nodded, "it is done." He reached for a bottle under his soiled jacket, opened it and handed it to Clemente. He had bought and sold land for a long time, and he understood what the separation meant to a man like Clemente. They both took long drinks of the warm, red wine.

"Clemente," don José mumbled, "I wish you luck in Albuquerque. I meant no disrespect, hombre, I only spoke of what I have seen happen. The sons grow to be men, they forget the old ways——"

Clemente nodded. He understood what the old man said. It was that fear of losing the stability he had always known that had kept him from making the move many years before. He had seen the changes and troubles that befell those up-rooted people who had left the land of their birth, and it had made him afraid. But without a job the debts had mounted until there was no more credit, and as his family grew they became more and more insistent about trying life elsewhere.

"¡Adiós! ¡Buena suerte! " Don José called, and his old truck rumbled away, back towards the town.

"It was necessary," Clemente shrugged. He squatted, picked up a handful of earth and let it sift through his fingers. "Somehow we began to lose the land a long time ago. The tejano came, the barbed wire came, the new laws came. A few survived, but death came and took so many of our family in such a short time——" He shook his head. "The three of us could have made it, Guillermo and Moisés and I, we could have made it, but after Guillermo was murdered it seemed that Moisés and I weren't strong enough to hold on——"

He felt his wife touch his shoulder. "You did not fail us, Clemente. It was Moisés who squandered away the ranch after el abuelo Chávez died. He drank and gambled away everything the Chávez family had worked for. We can be thankful that we still have our familia around us, Clemente. It is for them that we move, it is for them that we make the sacrifice."

She had witnessed the dissolution of the Chávez family after the grandfather Chávez died. Without his guiding hand to run the ranch, Moisés lost everything in less than a year's time, and Guillermo was tragically killed over a woman who was not worth one of his poems, or one of his enchanting smiles. So to save her familia Adelita had forced Clemente to salvage what little he could and move to Guadalupe where there was schooling available for her children. Now her daughters were grown, Juanita had just graduated from high school and Ana would finish in a year. They argued that opportunity and their future lay in the bigger city, and she agreed. She implored and finally convinced Clemente that the move was for the good of the family, and because a great deal of his faith rested in keeping his familia together he consented to pull up his roots and move.

"Sí, it is for the family," Clemente agreed. He stood and looked at the land and then he turned his gaze heavenward.

The sun hung like a gold medallion in the blue sky.

A cool breeze blew from the south and cooled his skin. Its soft caress evoked memories of the day he buried his son. He remembered every detail of that sorrowful day. He remembered the squeaking of the horse-drawn wagons that brought the mourners to the lonely grave in the llano, he remembered the faces of his vecinos and compadres as they lowered the casket into the grave, and he recalled the last rites of the priest. He remembered how the mourners parted, as it if were a part of a play well rehearsed, as he led the horse that had trampled and killed his oldest son to the edge of the grave. His compadre Campos had handed him the pistol. There was a flash of fire, then the loud report of the pistol echoing across the llano, like the sound of a tolling bell.

Campanas del llano . . . ¡Grítenme piedras su secreto!

The horse buckled and tumbled into the fresh grave, then his compadres helped him fill the grave and plant a small piñon tree over it.

Yes, the sun had been like that, like a gold medallion in the Indian-turquoise sky.

"Juanita and Ana are ready," Adelita murmured.

"They've been ready for hours," Benjie laughed. "They've been sitting in the truck since we finished packing——" He turned and walked towards the truck without a last goodbye.

Adelita stood by her husband and looked at the house. "It seems haunted already," she whispered. "People are the soul of a

6

home, when they depart they leave behind an empty skeleton——"

"Every adobe, every nail, every board contains a memory," Clemente added.

"We will build a new home," she smiled and tried to be brave, "And with it will come a new future."

She understood her husband's apprehension. The money from the sale of their home would barely pay off the debts, then they would be alone and broke in a new city. Her family and old neighbors and relatives would be left behind. Their families had lived in this land for many generations, now they were tearing themselves away from it. It was not easy, but she had resolved to do it for her sons and daughters. She took courage from that.

"We can build a new home," Clemente nodded, "but can we take the spirit of the land with us? "

" ¡Sí! " she answered forcefully. From the discarded pile of trash she picked up an empty coffee can and filled it with earth from her flower garden. "We will take it with us," she smiled and handed him the can. "Our land is everywhere," she said, "we will journey across the earth, but we will never leave our land——"

. . . centuries before, the brown hands of an Indian woman had scooped the earth of the heartland into a clay vessel, like the ashes that remain of the man are poured into the urn, and the people had carried that sacred urn as they wandered across the new land to complete their destiny. The earth was the new covenant between the people and their gods——

He took the can and smiled. He wished he could carry in this can, filled with his beloved earth, the spiritual connection he felt for the llano and the river valley. But just as he was sure the love for the land could not be transferred on a piece of paper, he knew he could not carry his attachment in the canful of simple, good earth. He was afraid of being separated from the rhythm of the heartbeat of the land.

He did not relish the journey, but he called out, " ¡Vamos! "
"Alabados sean los dulces nombres," Adelita blessed their journey, and the stain of dark earth marked the corners of the cross on her forehead and bosom.

"Jasón," Clemente turned to his son, "you also leave much behind. The old man——" He looked into his son's eyes and realized that he was not the only one who hurt at parting.

Jason nodded but did not speak.

"I am sorry," Clemente whispered and climbed into the truck.

"We're ready! " Ana cried excitedly.

Jason and Benjie climbed on top of the furniture in the back. They checked everything and called down, " ¡Está bien! ¡Vamos! "

"Have we left anything behind? " Adlita was still worrying about the possessions through which she had sorted, wondering if she had made the right choice on what to take and what to leave behind.

"Not a darn thing," Juanita said and breathed a sigh of relief, "just a small town with no future in it——"

"Yeah," Ana agreed. Juanita was right. Juanita was eighteen, just graduated from high school, and she knew everything. She turned and whispered to her sister, "Only a few boyfriends——"

"Bah! " Juanita laughed. "Boys is right! Gas station attendants who can only take care of the needs of the travelers, but who are trapped because they can never travel themselves. But we are not trapped, and where we go there'll be some real men——"

"We leave a lifetime behind," Adelita said, "but that past has been like a dream. Now we move into a new future——"

"We leave the land and the dead," Clemente whispered, and he turned the truck into highway 66 and headed westward.

They moved out of the green river valley, away from Guadalupe surrounded by its stagnant waters which no longer whispered to the time of innocence and childhood. They journeyed out of the land of the eagle and the nopal and headed westward, towards the thin, blue outline of the mountain range. If they had looked back they would have seen the town of Guadalupe disappear in the shimmering mirage of water that surrounded it, but they didn't look because they were afraid that as the town disappeared into the hills something in it would call them back. They looked ahead, always keeping in sight the mountains that marked their destination, never looking at the strange, green oasis that appeared and disappeared in the floating waters of the heat waves.

By mid-afternoon they entered the cañon that cut through the Sandía mountains. They marveled at the huge boulders that stood guard on either side of the highway, giant sentries marked with the cryptic signs of those who had gone before them. As they topped a rise they could see the valley spread below them. It was a lush, green snake, winding its way along the spine of the Rockies and here at the coccyx it dropped into the desert to the south. The city of Albuquerque lay nestled along the river, with the mountains guarding her eastern door and ancient volcano cones as sentries at her western gate. And so the mountain had parted to allow them a glimpse of their new valley, their new home.

"Por el amor de Dios——" Adelita sighed and crossed herself. It was only a few hours journey, but it had seemed a lifetime in the making, and she wondered what fate this new city held for them.

"¡Miren! ¡Miren! " Clemente shouted, and then he added, "You know that the first Chávezes were from this valley. Before they went to settle in the llano of Guadalupe, they lived here! " He felt excited.

"My God, it's big! " Juanita exclaimed. The city seemed to spread along the valley as far as she could see.

"We'll get lost——" Ana murmured.

"Oh no," Adelita said confidently, "we have Roberto's instructions on how to get there." She opened the letter she had clutched in her hand throughout the trip. "We're supposed to go straight ahead," she read, "straight into town until we get to 4th street . . ."

Clemente nodded and guided the truck down the main street, past the endless motels and gas stations until they reached the downtown area. All the streets seemed to lead into that small area of congestion. He dipped into the underpass beneath the railroad tracks and came up into thick five o'clock traffic and throngs of workers. For a moment he was bewildered.

"Where——" he turned anxiously.

"Straight ahead," Adelita motioned, "don't turn until we find 4th street! That will take us to Barelas! Everyone look for the street! " She commanded.

"We passed 1st! There's 2nd! " Benjie shouted from on top the furniture.

They crept through the heavy traffic, lost in the melee of the afternoon rush, bewildered by the snarl of confusion that surrounded them. At the corner of 4th where the traffic was heaviest a newspaper boy called, "R-rrread all about it! Explosion kills two in railroad yards! " And at the same time Adelita shouted,

"There's 4th! " And Clemente made an illegal turn south in search of Barelas.

The barrio was a welcome place to drive into that afternoon. The summer afternoon air was thick with dust that rose from the feet of children playing and from the workers who trudged down the dusty streets. The dust swirled in clouds behind pachuco-laden cars, and it covered the sweating boys of the barrio who played baseball in the street. The dust settled over the towering elms and the house tops of Barelas like a veil pulled by the golden fingers of the afternoon sun.

To Jason, perched atop the furniture, Barelas Road was like a meandering river, winding its way through the barrio until it met the river at the Barelas Bridge. There the barrio ended. Jason listened. The soft melody of a guitar seemed to draw him close to their final destination. Around him children called and ran to meet their fathers; neighbors visited across fences and paused in their small talk to turn to wave at the new arrivals. Smiles were in the soft air, and so was the fragrance of roasting chile verde and hot tortillas, supper for the hungry workers. The air was heavy with the damp smell of just-watered gardens, dirty with the bad smell of sewage that drifted up from the sewage plant in south Barelas, and acrid with the salty sweat-smell of the grimy workers from the railroad yard.

At times the air bristled with the static of the pachucos, the zoot-suiters who went swinging down the street as if they owned it, speaking a strange, mysterious argot. Jason motioned at Benjie, but he didn't have to because Benjie was already looking, already entranced with the finger-snapping, duck-tailed chucos that Roberto had called los vatos locos in his letters from Barelas. "Hey man," he heard Benjie whisper, "that's cool——"

At a place where the street widened and seemed to pause momentarily in its flow to form a wide pond, Clemente stopped the car to ask for directions. Across the street was a woodyard and several men were gathered there, neighbors exchanging news in that pause before supper. They drank beer and relaxed and talked about work at the railroad yard where most of the men from

10

Barelas worked. They turned when Clemente approached them; they had seen the packed, decrepit truck coming and they guessed they would have new neighbors. The man who owned the woodyard, a heavy-set, strong man approached Clemente. They exchanged buenas tardes.

"I am Manuel," the old man said. They shook hands.

"Clemente Chávez . . . I am looking for my son, Roberto. Perhaps you know where he lives . . ."

"Sonamagon, sure I know Roberto, everybody here knows Roberto. He's a good boy . . . Hey! " he turned and shouted at the men, "This is our new vecino! He's Roberto's father! " The men drew forward and shook hands with Clemente and introduced themselves.

"And look," old Manuel pointed and Clemente turned to see Roberto bounding across the street. He opened the truck door and swept his mother out in an embrace, "You came to ask directions and you came right to the place. Roberto lives right across the street, and I think the house he has rented for you is the one Jesús Sena left when he moved . . ."

"Jesús Sena? " Clemente asked, "Isn't he the man from Milagro? "

"Yes, the same one," Manuel nodded.

"Well, I knew him once, when he worked at Las Lagrimas," Clemente said, and as they talked about the people they knew they found many neighbors and compadres in common and Clemente realized that many of the families he had known in the small towns and ranchos were now here in the city.

Roberto and his wife Rita, who was heavy with their first child, finished greeting everyone and Roberto approaced his father and embraced him. "Apá, I am glad to see you. Was it a good trip? Any trouble on the road? "

"No, no problems," Clemente answered happily, "we drove slowly, and here we are. We came right to the place——"

"He stopped to ask for directions and he didn't know he was here," old Manuel smiled.

"Yes, this is the right place," Roberto beamed proudly and he looked at the small crowd that had gathered to see the new family that was moving in. "——This is Barelas," he said, "this is our barrio." And the people nodded silently.

11

"We are glad to be here," Adelita said, "I am happy because my familia is together again——" and she embraced them all then wiped the tears from her eyes and said, "it is the will of God."

"Roberto, show them the place," Rita prodded him.

"Yes, yes, follow me. It's right across the street, very close to our house, and right in the middle of the barrio. Right here, we say, is the heart of Barelas . . . everybody that comes new into the city comes here——" He put one arm around Rita and one around his mother and walked with them. To Jason and Benjie he said, "I'm glad to see you two indios . . . you'll like it here. In a while we'll go over and visit Crispín, maybe later on we'll go watch the Dukes play . . ." He was excited and happy.

Clemente turned to Manuel and thanked him; he was happy to have the woodcutter for a neighbor. "Ah, it's nothing," old Manuel shrugged, "come on, We'll help you move the heavy pieces of furniture——" He motioned and the men followed. They parked the truck by the house and very quickly had it unloaded, then the men silently drifted away, each to his own family and supper. They knew the new man would need time to settle down; now they simply told Clemente if he needed anything they were willing to help. As they left they called out, "Hasta luego, vecino."

The inconvenience of the disorder of moving in was lightened by the excitement they felt. With the furniture moved in, Juanita and Ana could make beds while Adelita and Rita prepared the first supper in the new home. Rita had cooked a pot of beans for them and now they only made fresh tortillas. Dorotea, old Manuel's wife, brought them a big bowl of natillas and hot coffee. She was a round, gay woman, always ready with a colorful story, and she quickly took to Adelita and her family. After she left Rita said she and Manuel had been very good to her and Roberto but that doña Dorotea made her nervous because she was forever patting Rita on the stomach and saying she would make her husband proud with that precious load she was carrying. They laughed and ate supper on unpacked boxes and crates. When they were done Juanita and Ana hurried to wash the dishes so they could go outside and sit on the fence to watch the young men of the barrio who strolled up and down the street. Adelita and Rita continued the unpacking and Roberto invited Jason and Benjie to Crispín's to hear the old man play his guitar.

"Nah, not me," Benjie winked, "there's a lot of action in the street. I want to get into it——"

"Be careful," Roberto warned him, "most of that action can get you into a lot of trouble."

"Listen to Roberto," Clemente nodded, "he has been here long enough to know. Stay away from bad company."

"Apá," Benjie grinned and went to his father, "I'm not going to get into any trouble, I'm just going to look. Bueno? " He placed his hand on his father's shoulder and Clemente had to nod and say bueno. Benjie went out whistling.

"I swear that boy isn't afraid of the devil himself," Clemente shook his head. He had looked out at the swirl of activity in the street and had retreated; he was content to sit on the back steps after supper. Here it was quiet and peaceful. Across the valley he could hear the sounds of the guitar. The man they called Crispín was playing old melodies.

"Well, the devil rides fancy cars out there," Roberto tossed his head towards the street, "and he sells junk. Marijuana, mota the pachucos call it, and worse stuff——"

Clemente felt uneasy. He turned to call his son, but Benjie was gone. "Well," he said, "let's go listen to this poet of the barrio . . ."

Roberto led them across the alley. He pushed open an old wooden gate and they entered a lush green garden. The cool air was rich and spermy with the smell of earth. "He's got magic in his fingers," Roberto whispered, "for plants and for the strings . . ."

The porch of the small adobe held four of the men of the vicinity. They clustered around an old man who sat under the dim farole light and strummed his guitar. The guitar was blue, a glowing blue under the soft light, it semed alive under the old man's touch. He paused and turned slightly. His blind eyes searched the darkness.

"Roberto! " he called cheerfully, "ah, how good to hear your footsteps. Come in, come in, find a chair——" He paused again and listened. "And your father. He's with you. He arrived. Good, very good." He stood and held out his hand. Clemente took it and felt the strong clasp of the old man, and he felt a strange power of recognition flow from the musician. Clemente thought he knew the poet and he looked intently at him, but Crispín's eyes were

13

clouded with cataracts.

"And this is my brother," Roberto said.

"Ah, the one you said is named Jasón, eh." He took Jason's hand. "So, you and you father have come from Guadalupe to try your luck in this city. Well, it will be good," he nodded, but there was a ring of sadness in his voice. He bent and whispered in Jason's ear, "Someday we will talk about a friend of yours I knew from Guadalupe . . ." He smiled and pulled back and Jason was left with a humming in his ears. It was the same sound he had often heard in the hills of Guadalupe, in the evening when he was far from home and he thought he heard the old Indian calling him. He always stopped and turned to listen intently and then the sound would disappear and he could hear his heart beating. Once, he remembered, Anthony had told him that he too heard and felt that sound when he touched the old woman who could fly.

"Now sit, sit anywhere, make yourselves at home," Crispín said. "There's hot coffee on the stove, and Primo has a little wine bottle he is willing to share." Everyone laughed and Primo's flat, brown face got red. He stood and shook Clemente's hand and then they took a drink together and became friends.

"Now play us a song," Roberto entreated.

"Play us a song of love," another man said, "of things as they are . . ."

Crispín smiled and said, "Things as they are never appear the same on the blue guitar . . . For as ten fingers can nimbly play across the strings and make a hundred variations, the imagination has a million fingers that constantly reshape things as they are . . ." And he hunched over the blue guitar and drew out the sweet music and as they listened each man's mind wandered through his own world and shaped and reshaped the substance of his memories. That was the power of Crispín's guitar, that and the fact that some men said its music could stop death in his tracks, and some swore that it could stop time because when the melody was over you did not remember that you had been sitting an hour or two and that during that time your thoughts had wandered in the eternity of the moment. Time stood still. The magic music stirred the soul. The wine warmed the blood. Each man traveled where he would on the chords of the blue guitar. And when it was done they stood and thanked Crispín.

14

"I swear that music soothes my tired muscles," one said.

"It makes life worthwhile," his friend added as they stepped into the garden and disappeared in the darkness, calling out their buenas noches y mañana el trabajo.

"My old woman always knows when I've stopped off at Crispín's," the big man said, "because I can love so well after listening to the blue guitar! " And he shouted a grito full of life; it echoed down the streets of the barrio. He went out dancing, "It makes me want to laugh and sing, ai-ee-ee . . ." And those that remained joined in his laughter. They remained because after his playing Crispín or one of the old men of the barrio would tell a story. Tonight one of the men asked Crispín about the old woman who lived in one of the dark pockets of the barrio near the irrigation canal.

"Is it true that cursed rock of hers contains magic? " the man asked.

"They say she tells fortunes . . . she can predict when you will die, or if you will come into money . . ." another added.

"La piedra mala," Primo shook his head, "that evil rock is bad business; keep away from it."

"But they say it can sing, like Crispín's guitar, but more than that, it can talk. It knows the secrets of a man's heart! "

"Ay, if you sell your soul to its darkness . . ." Primo cautioned.

"Bah! Sometimes things get so bad that what does it matter if that evil rock owns your soul or the goddamned railroad yard! Either way a poor man is damned! "

The others nodded. That was true. Jason leaned forward to listen. He was surpsied to hear the story of the singing rocks repeated here. A long time ago the Indian had told him the story of these magic rocks. They had much power because they were part of the gods' gifts to the people at the time they settled by the river. Clemente also listened. He had heard many stories in the llano, but never one about la piedra mala. He, too, felt it strange that he had come to this little pool in the river of Barelas to listen to the story.

"I have often thought of visiting the old woman! " one of the impetuous young men boasted.

"Yeah, but you never got past the house of las Golondrinas, las putas! " His friend slapped him on the back and they laughed at

15

him.

"I mean I wouldn't be afraid! " he defended himself.

"But why would you go to visit la India, the old woman who keeps the black rock? " Crispín asked.

The young man searched for an answer. "I, I don't know . . ." he mumbled, "but sometimes a person gets depressed, he has nowhere to turn . . . It's like Héctor just said, if you have no job and your kids are going hungry then it doesn't matter if you sell your soul to the devil or to the railroad! Either way, we're in the same pinch all the time, just holding our noses above debts so we won't drown, hoping things at the shops don't get worse and hoping el Super doesn't shut off our credit at the store . . . well, it's times like that when a man in desperation will turn to something like la piedra mala! "

"But it's a magic rock! " Jason blurted. "It's not evil, it's only those who use it that are evil——" He stopped short and settled back, uneasy with the silence he created in the room.

"True," Crispín nodded, "the black singing rocks were once kept by priests, and on them they carved the calendar of time . . . history sleeps in their web . . ." he sighed. "There is power in that magic rock, and men go to it for different things——"

"Have you ever talked to la piedra? " one of the men asked. The question was direct, but that was the way they talked to the old man and there was no disrespect intended. Crispín turned to Clemente as if he had asked the question. "I talk to my blue guitar," he smiled, "and it talks to me . . ." He cradled the guitar and strummed a soft melody, and the guitar purred a lullaby of day's end. Slowly the men got up and drifted away. In the garden the orchestra of the night crickets complemented the waves of music that lapped against the shores of the barrio.

"A strange man," Clemente said to his son as they walked home.

"No stranger than Jason's Indian," Roberto answered. In the darkness he said to Jason, "I am sorry he died the way he died . . ."

Jason didn't answer. The Indian had said not to grieve. He rested in the sealed cave above the River of the Carp. They were building a dam there now, and soon everything would be covered with water, again.

16

In their back yard they found old Manuel, who had come, he said, "a dar gracias y las buenas noches." He held up a bottle of cold wine. "There is a lot to celebrate, eh Roberto, your parents are here, safe and sound. That is good. I think for that we can all get up a little later tomorrow morning."

"The devil's shops don't allow for celebrations of home-coming," Roberto smiled. "We'll all have to be there on time tomorrow morning. But there's time for one drink——" They sat on the wooden steps of the back door and Manuel opened the bottle. Jason continued inside. The house was quiet and dark. He found the small room in the back that had been designated for him and Benjie and undressed. He lay down and thought for a long time about the things the old poet had said tonight and how they connected with many of the things the Indian had said. Somehow there were threads that interwove in and out of the old stories, but tonight he was too tired and the summer heat too stifling for him to find the answer. He turned his attention to listening to the men outside.

"I can't see the stars from here," he heard his father say.

"It is because of the city lights around us," Manuel explained.

"In the summer nights of the llano the stars and the moon are constant companions——"

"Papá," Roberto put his hand on his father's shoulder, "you'll get used to it. This is a new place——"

"It is a good place, Roberto, you found us a good home. There is a big back yard here, perhaps we can keep some animals, some chickens, maybe a pig," he said cheerfully.

"No," Manuel said, "no animals. There is a city ordinance against keeping animals——"

"But why?" Clemente asked.

"Who knows," old Manuel shrugged. "They say the animals smell, but they keep the sewage plant in South Barelas and we have to live with the stench when the breeze blows north—— The laws are passed by the politicos in City Hall, and so they can call one smell a nuisance to public health and the other a necessity. Either way, they don't have to live with it, they all live up in the heights or across the park in the Country Club."

"I see," Clemente nodded. He felt at ease with the old man. "Can't a man even keep a garden?" he asked.

17

"A jardín? Sure," Manuel said. "Why sonamagon, there already is one, over there in the corner where the sun can shine through the elms. Jesús, who lived here before you, he kept a good garden. Since he left I have tried to water it as often as I could, but it needs a lot of work, the weeds are taking it over——"

They walked through the green garden where the grillos sang their summer song. It was cool where the rows of chile, tomatoes, squash and corn had been watered.

"All of the people who come to the city keep a garden," old Manuel said, "it is some rememberance of home we bring with us, and try to keep. A man must work the earth with his hands, he must keep in touch with it, or else he forgets. God pity those who forget——"

"It is true," Clemente said, and when the old man had gone he went into the house and found the can full of earth entrusted to him by his wife. He scattered the earth of his llano over his new piece of land. He mixed the old earth of his valley into the hard city soil, and in the dark green of the night his hands dug into the earth as he sought some reassurance from the dark web of his sleeping mother.

The night air was full of strange sounds. Somwhere a siren wailed, and for a moment they thought they heard the cry of la Llorona as she ran along the dark river valley, crying for her demon-lover, mourning the death of her sons. But no, this was a new llorona! It was the siren of a police car crying through the streets of the barrio, searching out the young men who possessed the magic plant of summer, marijuana.

You cannot flee from me, it cried, I seek you out in all new lands. I am the essence of your smoke, I am the spirit of your past.

At the railroad shops the trains screamed as they came roaring into the yard to be serviced by the graveyard shift. A distant rumbling filled the dark and erupted in thunder and flashes of fire. Even at night the trains would not rest, they thrashed about like snakes in a pit and demanded service. Humble men, shadows of the night, moved to do their bidding.

They listened to the new sounds and tried to let fatigue lead them to sleep, but their excitement would not allow death's brother to carry them to his time of forgetfulness. In their room Juanita and Ana whispered.

"What are you thinking? " Ana asked.

"I don't know," Juanita answered, "I guess I'm just thinking how free I feel——"

"Yeah, me too. Did you notice all the neat guys that came by to talk to Roberto? Wow, are they cool! "

"Uh-huh," Juanita murmured and drifted to sleep.

In their room at the back of the house Benjie rolled a cigarette and talked to Jason. "Man, this place is really alive! Like those pachucos we saw this afternoon, they're all over. I walked down to the street light on the corner and I told them I'm Roberto's brother, and right away they treat me okay. The vatos here are a toda madre! " he exclaimed. "They even offered me a smoke of marijuana, a toke they call it. 'Come on, ése, you're one of us, take a toke,' one of the vatos said. I did, and I tried to breathe it like I saw them breathing, and I choked——" Benjie laughed to himself. He struck the match to light his cigarette and for a moment Jason could see his brother's face.

"Roberto said to be careful with that stuff," Jason said.

"Ah, what does Roberto know," Benjie smiled. "You know how Roberto is, Jason, and now that he's married he's even more serious than he used to be. But I bet he had his fun while he was in Korea, now it's our turn! I don't want anybody around telling me what to do and what not to do——"

"He's not telling you, Benjie, he just said be careful."

"Yeah, well I'm going to be careful," Benjie lay back on his bed and blew smoke rings in the dark, "but I'm going to have me some fun too——" He thought Jason would respond and when he didn't Benjie continued, "You know what, Jason, you're kinda like Roberto, serious, quiet—you got moods like a poet. In fact, all of you are like that, except me, the only thing I want out of life is fun——" He crumpled the cigarette butt in the ashtray and the room was dark and quiet.

In the nest of their new bed Clemente stroked the brown, soft flesh of his wife's stomach. She was still a fruitful woman, but she guarded very carefully the rhythms of her moon. He understood why. She had been the first to see the mangled body of their son when the horse dragged him in, and she still remembered. Life became a serious thing that tragic afternoon, the joy of youth left her eyes, and she guarded the life she produced jealously. Sometimes, he thought, with too much effort, but then perhaps only those who had created and nurtured a life could understand and feel the depths of *la tristeza de la vida.*

"Are you asleep? " he asked her.

"No——" she murmured.

"What are you thinking? " He asked in the dark.

"About our new life," she answered, "and the fact that this winter we will be grandparents, imagine me, an abuelita——" She laughed softly. "I don't know where the time has gone——"

"It has not been so bad," he laughed back, and she responded to his caresses, like the earth had answered his touch.

"A new life coming," she moaned to his love-rhythm, "and they say that there must be a death to balance it——"

He sensed something ominous in her words and felt her nails dig into his flesh. He wanted to stay awake and talk into the night and try to understand how she felt about their new home, but when their brown, sweating bodies parted she was instantly asleep. He lay awake for a long time, vaguely resentful that their love could bring her such sound sleep while it only brought questions to his mind.

Who is the woman sleeping by my side. Did we meet and love in some foreign country, or in the time of our youth, or in some dream?

And what of the future, he thought. And for a long time his thoughts would not let him rest.

Finally, sleep did come. The pulse of the barrio slowed and sleep crept into its lifestream. The grillos droning in the trees and the soft sound of Crispín's guitar lulled it to sleep.

CHAPTER TWO

"¡Levántense! ¡Levántense! " Adelita cried as she shook her daughters. She had let them sleep late because yesterday had been a long, hard day, but now there was the house to be cleaned and straightened and groceries to buy.

"Mamá! Por favor," Juanita groaned.

"Just five more minutes," Ana pleaded.

"Five more minutes, válgame Dios, but you would sleep all day if I let you! " She swept the sheets off them and then hurried into the kitchen, calling Jason and Benjie as she went.

"Aquí, mamá," Jason answered.

"Benjamín? " she asked.

"Still sleeping——"

"¡Por Dios Santo! " She shook her head, "They wanted to come to the city, now they are here and sleeping their time away! " She served Jason his breakfast. Jason mixed Carnation milk into the steaming atole and sprinkled sugar on it.

"Roberto took your father to the railroad yard with him, and he has not returned. Blessed be God and all the saints, but I am sure he has gotten work! Oh, what a miracle if he has gotten a job on the first day! It's almost noon and he hasn't returned, surely that means he got a job, and he will need some lunch. You will have to run and take him some lunch——"

Jason hastily swallowed the last of the cereal. He took the faded lunch pail she handed him.

"You can't get lost," she went on, "walk straight down Barelas Road, it will take you to the shops . . . when you get there ask for your father, or ask for Roberto, someone will know him. Dios te bendiga——" She reached out and touched his forehead and he turned and ran out into the bright day. He looked up at the white sun and realized he had slept very late, but that was because he had not been able to fall asleep for a long time. A few cars crept up the dusty street, otherwise the barrio was still and empty. In one yard two women hung their wash and gossiped across the fence. They turned to watch Jason walking down the middle of the road.

Jason did not see them. His eyes were fixed on the huge, round water tank that rose out of the dark buildings at the end of the road. It towered above the barrio, so that Jason could read the letters on the faded cross. SANTA FE. The black tower of steel loomed over everything. Around it trains thrashed like giant serpents, and when they coupled the monstrous act gave unnatural birth to chains of steel. Jason cautiously approached the labyrinth of grimy buildings, steel tracks and boxcars. The houses near the yards were dark with soot and the elm trees withered and bare. A chain link fence surrounded the yards. Jason found the gate just when a blast of steam shook him from his daydream. The silence was ripped open by thunder and lightning that spewed out of the dark forge.

"My God! " Jason cried, and at that moment a hand grabbed his shoulder and he was spun around. He looked up into the white, rolling eyes of a giant man.

"Wha'cha wan' here, boy? " the grimy man's voice thundered above the noises of the shops.

"My father! " Jason shouted, "I'm looking for my father! " He tried to squirm loose but it was useless.

The gate-man roared with laughter. "Hey boy! 'Das a thasand men in 'dis devil's place! Any one of dem could be yoor daddy! " He leered and scratched at his crotch. "—— 'cept me! " he added and laughed again. "Wha'cha got 'der, huh? " He pointed at the lunch pail.

"It's lunch, for my father——" Jason pulled back but the big man had grabbed the pail. He tore it open and scowled, "Friggin' lunch! Das all, jus' a friggin' lunch! " He took the sweet raisin bread Adelita had baked that morning and tossed the pail back at Jason. "Go un, kid, go fin' yoor old man, but don' go fin' eem dead and trip over him, huh! " He laughed again and at the same time he stuffed the sweet roll into his huge mouth.

Jason turned and disappeared quickly into the boxcar canyons.

22

He felt his heart pounding and he laughed to himself. The big man had shaken him; he hadn't been so frightened in a long time. Now he turned and wandered into the maze the gate-man had called the devil's place. Around him gangs of men cursed and worked in the mid-day heat. Jason watched for his father or Roberto but there was no sign of them. He circled and started back when he spotted a man that looked like his father. He stood beneath a huge, steel crane, working with the crew that were flexed to push a boxcar away from the crane dock.

"Papá! " Jason called, but his shout was drowned out by the man who called, "Come on, raza! One big push and she's done! " The man was not his father, but still Jason felt rooted to the spot. Out of the corner of his eye he had seen the tangled wire on top of the car catch the huge chain that hung from the crane. The men grunted and pushed and as the car moved forward it pulled the heavy chain and stretched it in an arc.

"All together, raza! We can do it! "

"This car is as slow as my mother in law! " one of them joked.

"La pinche mala suerte herself! " another cursed.

The car suddenly lurched forward and the men jumped back, but they didn't see the heavy chain stretched out. The wire that had caught the chain snapped and the chain came swinging back.

" ¡Cuidao! " Jason shouted, and the man turned to catch a glimpse of the shadow swinging at him.

" ¡Sánchez! " one of the workers called in horror. He had heard the wire snap and he turned in time to see the chain swing back at Sánchez.

Both warnings were too late. Sánchez turned his head as if to ward off the blow and at that instant the iron hook on the end of the chain hit him squarely on the side of the head and cracked open his skull. The impact flipped him in the air.

The gods had demanded blood and now it bathed the sun in red .

Sánchez cried out once, as if to protest the cowardly way death had leaped from the bright sun to end his life, and when he hit the ground he quivered like an animal that had been shot. His friends leaped forward to help, but it was already too late. They pulled him away from beneath the chain which was still swinging like a giant pendulum.

23

"¡Hijo de la chingada! " One of them cursed and turned away.

Jason, too, had leaped forward. He looked down at the bloodied face and heard himself scream. At the same time the shrill blast of the noon whistle exploded and drowned his cry. It was twelve o'clock and the sun paused to witness the shadow of death it had left on a man.

"Somebody better go for an ambulance! "

"It's too late, goddamit! He's dead! He's dead! "

They looked helplessly at the man that a few moments ago had been alive, a man they had known and worked with for so many years and who was now stretched out at their feet. They cursed their impotency in the face of death and when they looked up and saw the swarm of workers who had come running to see what had happened they could only shrug and turn away. One of the workers placed his hand on Jason's shoulder and asked, "Did you know him? I heard you call him——"

"No! " Jason cried. He felt his head pounding and he heard the surge of a swollen river at its summer flood. He wanted to pull the man away from that sound that was rushing away, but he didn't know how. Around him the workers pressed forward to ask questions. One of them knelt by the body and in disbelief kept repeating, "Oh my God, it's Sánchez! It's Sánchez! " He put his rough, calloused hands to his face and wept.

"Has anyone called the priest? "

"Damn, it's too late now . . . it's too late now. He was alive a minute ago, and now it's too late . . . ¡Ay que pinche mala suerte! " the man cried as if in agony.

"All morning we had trouble with that car, and it ends like this! " another cursed in frustration.

"It's nobody's fault, hombre," his friend tried to reassure him, "his time had come. Ya le tocaba . . ."

"No one's to blame . . . It was just bad luck . . ."

"Those sons of bitches up there are to blame! " Another worker shouted and jumped forward. He shook an angry fist at the blank faces that looked down on the death scene from the offices atop the yard administration. "Sánchez's work crew had been cut back twice! It's unsafe to work with so few men! You all know that! Yes, someone's to blame, and the blame lies with those bastards that treat us like animals and our rotten union that won't protect us! " He cursed again and swore that he wouldn't forget the death of Sánchez. The men nodded in agreement.

"Lalo's right," another said, "last month it was Juan, he lost all his fingers when a wheel slipped. He should've had help! And now this! "

An older man stepped forward and said, "Now is not the time to curse the bosses or the union . . . If we are men and not animals, let us first take care of our dead . . ." He had brought an oily tarp with which he covered the body because the sun was hot and the flies were already swarming. They lowered their heads and prayed in silence. The zia sun in its zenith beat mercilessly on their backs. The shop whistle began a mournful cry, alerting the women of the barrio that death had taken one of their men. The dusty barrio streets filled with the black shawls of death as the women hurried towards the shops, each one praying to la Virgen de Guadalupe that it not be her husband or son, and each one lamenting the pain of death that already eroded the heart.

The women arrived and encircled the body. Already they knew who the man was beneath the tarp, and so they whispered their prayers and their Ave Marias to speed him to God. Then the ancient, dark cry of mourning exploded from the soul of the woman who had lost her husband, like the terrifying scream of a wounded animal she raised her voice to heaven and pleaded with God to let her husband live again.

" ¡Dios mío! ¡Dios mío! " She pounded her breast and raised her arms to heaven.

. . . there had been times of darkness, four times the earth and its life had been consumed in the void, and each time the blood of sacrifice had raised the light. Now the fifth sun, a blinding, white deer raced across the sky; a new legend would have to be told, a new myth created before the deer gave its power to the people.

Her daughters gathered around her and lent their tears to the day. The women of the barrio consoled the widow and shared her anguish.

" ¡Dios mío! " they cried to God to turn death back, but it was too late. Sánchez's wife had torn away the tarp and cradled her husband's body in her arms. " ¡Dios mío! " she cried, " ¡Dios mío! Give me back my husband! Do not let him die! Take me! Take me! But do not let him die! " The men pulled her away and gave her to the women so they would comfort her in her grief, and then they covered the body again because it was already too late to ask for life.

The men shuffled their feet and looked at each other helplessly. Somewhere a siren wailed and mixed its cry into the anguish of the women. A cool breeze rippled through the crowd and they shivered. One of the young workers standing next to Jason whispered, "Well, there's nothing we can do here . . . we better go eat."

"Yeah," his buddy nodded, "let's go eat in the shade of the water tank . . . it's cool there . . ."

"I feel sorry for Sánchez," the worker said as they walked away, "but he's dead now . . . and at one o'clock when the whistle blows that pinche foreman's gonna want us on the job, or you get on report and tomorrow it's no job . . ."

Jason watched them walk away. He could not accept death as easily as they. Something in the mournful cries of the women and the wailing siren had touched a chord of memory. He remembered what the Indian had said about a song that could touch the stream of life and death, and suddenly Crispín's name exploded in his dry throat and he knew there was something he could do.

With tears blinding his eyes Jason stumbled through the maze that was Barelas and somehow found his way to the alley that led to Crispín's hut. He pushed through the hanging vines, past the tall stalks of guardian corn, and into the house.

"Crispín! " He cried.

"Aquí mijo——" Crispín whispered and touched Jason.

Jason turned in the dark shadows of the room and looked into the old man's blind eyes, and at the same time he heard the pulse of an electric melody flash from the strings of the blue guitar. He fell backward, blinded by the glow from the guitar, reeling from the fragments of music which bounced from the walls of the room and echoed a resounding death knell. He reached out and held the old man.

"Play the song of life! " he gasped, "the secret melody! " He held Crispín tightly and tried to see beyond the white cataracts that covered the eyes like clouds covering the sun.

"It is too late," Crispín moaned, "the man is dead——"

"No! " Jason insisted, "You know it is never too late! Play now before his soul is gone! "

26

"My son, my son," Crispín held Jason and tried to comfort the angry, trembling boy, "it is too late ... the four winds have gathered, already they whisper a new song. It was that man's time to die!" he said firmly and held Jason. Jason looked at the strong, brown face webbed with the wrinkles of old age and nodded. He began to accept the death of Sánchez. "His death was too strong to turn back ... it rolled like a shadow and covered the barrio ..."

Jason felt his body go limp. Crispín had tried and there was nothing else to do. He could no longer hold back the sobs that had choked at his throat since he began to run. Now he cried freely and the convulsions of grief relieved him. Crispín held the boy while he cried, and his words comforted him. He told Jason how it was that sometimes death came so suddenly that it could not be turned back, and that even a man as old as he who had spent his life seeking death's riddle could not yet pluck the strings to make death cry. Then he sang and strummed the blue guitar.

"Aie-ee-ee, it is the wind that sings my song ..."

The lament filled the barrio and flowed into the *Padre Nuestro que estás en los cielos, santificado sea tu nombre* that the women prayed around the corpse; it mixed into the fiery tequila-grito that tore itself from the throats of friends as they remembered their dead compadre.

"Cou-cou-rou-coo-coo ..." He opened his soul and the pigeons that gathered on the church tower and the doves of the river responded to the dirge.

And when the song of death was done and death was drenched with tears they sat and talked. Jason told Crispín about the old Indian and Crispín nodded and said he had known that man from Guadalupe. Then he told Jason the story of the blue guitar.

When the flutes of the priests were broken and wise words no longer curled from the mouths of poets and philosophers, then the blue guitar was carved from the heart of a juniper tree. Its color was the blue of the mexican sky, its strings are rays of the golden sun. Wise men tuned it to tell the legends of the people, and in it were stored the myths of the past. It was a new instrument, a subterfuge, passing from poet to poet it wove the future out of things as they are ... so nothing could be destroyed, so everything could be created anew. It was there when the people arrived to carve the calendar-sun and it was there when the cross of Christ was driven into the flesh of earth . . .

"I was apprenticed forty years to the man who handed it to me . . . and some day I will pass it on. But a part of the history was missing, stories never recorded on the blue guitar. I had to search the past to find myself . . . At last I moved north from Mexico in search of the land the ancients called Aztlán . . . I crossed the burning desert where the sun burned away my sight . . . And so I have journeyed ever since, it was my master's wish. To travel back into time, I learned, is really only to find a spot where one can plumb the depths.

"Now I sing the songs of the past and the songs of the future, and the people listen, and as they listen each man and woman adds his piece, and the song grows fuller, it blossoms under this kind sun . . ."

"And the song for death, and the song for time? " Jason asked.

Crispín smiled. "That is a song for life," he said, "perhaps the whim of an old man . . . I've sought it for so long . . ."

The shadows lengthened across Crispín's garden. The day was dying. The church bells tolled and called the people to the evening rosary. Overhead a flock of pigeons winged towards the river to drink with the wild doves.

Jason rose and walked to the door. He did not know what to say, he only knew the death of Sánchez and the memories of wrapping the Indian in his winding sheet and then sealing the cave on the bluff of the river were easier to bear because of what Crispín had said. The rage and frustration he had felt in the face of death were no longer excessive emotions. He did not know if he understood everything Crispín had said, but he felt composed. He turned and thanked the old man, and then he walked across the gathering shadows of the garden.

The family had gathered at supper when he arrived.

" ¡Válgame Dios! " His mother cried anxiously. "Where have you been? Such a terrible thing that happened, and you've been gone all afternoon! ¡Vagamundo! Are you going to be like your brother Benjamín? Sit, eat——"

"Leave him alone, woman," his father interceded for him, "a boy has the right to explore the world. Why should he bother his head with the tragic things of life, he'll have plenty of time to

28

learn of that—— Anyway, the important thing is I have a job! " He raised his wine glass and toasted his good luck.

"Thanks to Roberto," Adelita said. She had finished serving everyone.

"Yes, but also thanks to Sánchez," Roberto added. "At one o'clock the foreman hired papá on that crew——"

"Roberto! " Adelita exclaimed, "How can you say that! Is that all a man's death means? One more job? " She shook her head sadly; she couldn't believe her oldest son had grown so calloused.

"I'm sorry, mamá," Roberto apologized, "I didn't mean it that way . . . Sánchez was a good man, and what happened today was a tragedy, but what the hell, there just aren't that many jobs around! A man has to take what he can get . . ."

"Roberto is right," Clemente agreed.

"Right after I got back from Korea there was a lot of work, now it's getting very bad. Jobs are scarce and there's talk of a recession . . ."

"It's hard to buy the things one needs and try to save to buy a home . . ." Rita agreed.

"Never mind that, tell us what happened? " Juanita asked.

"Well, I was working down the line," Roberto said, "and I had just lifted my welding mask and looked towards the Sánchez' crew when the chain hit him. I swear when that hook hit his skull it sounded like an explosion, and the blood spurted all over the place! " He ate while he talked.

"Roberto, por favor," Rita nudged him.

"Well they wanted to hear," Roberto answered. "Hey, Jason, you were there. What were you doing? "

"He went to take his father's lonche," Adelita exclaimed.

"Did you see it, Jason? " Ana asked excitedly.

"No," Jason answered, "I didn't see anything——" He lowered his head so he wouldn't have to explain anything, and he tried to eat but he couldn't.

"Go on! " Juanita urged Roberto.

"What more is there? " Roberto shrugged. "He was dead when he hit the ground. There was blood all over the place—— Pasa el arroz." He asked for the rice.

"The velorio is tonight," Ana cut in.

29

"Uh-huh," Rita nodded, "at Montoya's Mortuary."

"Ave María Purísima," Adelita crossed her forehead.

"Bueno, ya le tocaba," Roberto said. His time had come. It has his turn to die.

"No more morbid talk," Clemente said, "what has happened, has happened. The truth is I have a job, and as difficult as they say work is to find here in the city, we should be thankful. My familia shall not want——"

"Gracias a Dios."

There was a whistle outside, and Juanita and Ana glanced shyly through the open door. The two young men who had flirted with them at the store were standing by the gate.

"Mamá," Juanita asked excitedly, "can we go outside? " Adelita nodded and the two hurried out.

"Hey! " Clemente banged his fist on the table, "Since when do my daughters run to answer a whistle! "

"Clemente," Adelita tried to calm him, "there is no harm done, they will be right outside——"

"I don't care where they will be! Has the common courtesy of knocking at the door changed? "

"Things are different here," Adelita tried to explain.

"Meeting the man of the house is not different! Not here or anywhere—— No, you cannot go! " He shouted.

But it was too late, they were gone.

After supper Jason asked Benjie if he was going to the rosary for Sánchez, but Benjie shrugged and said he didn't know the man, and anyway, he was going out with some of the vatos to shoot some eight ball and drink beer. So Jason made his way alone up the dark alleys of Barelas towards the mortuary. He followed the hunched, silent shadows towards the gathering point. He slipped quietly into the chapel. He sat where he could watch the mourners pass in front of the casket. He saw them cross their foreheads and utter short prayers for the dead man, then they moved into the small room at the side where they gave el pésame to the bereaved family. He caught sight of the eldest of the dead man's daughters, a dark beauty whose oval face slept beneath her dark manta, beneath the mask of mourning.

Then they prayed, and as the priest led them from bead to bead each supplicant escaped into the world of his own private thoughts. The sonorous drone of the monotonous Hail Marys let each mind wander and enact its own encounter with death. Grief was like a mask over their faces.

The praying continued and the men slipped outside, rubbing stiffened knees, gathering to light cigarettes and recount the death of Sánchez.

"——He was a good man."

"A good worker."

"I still can't believe it, hombre, he'd been in the shops since he was a kid . . . He should've known better."

"Cuando te toca, te toca," another said simply.

"Yes," his friend agreed, "when it's your time to go it doesn't matter if it's the pinche mala suerte that takes you or la chingada madre, it's all the same."

"I still can't believe it, hombre," the man insisted and shook his head, "just last Saturday night I had a beer with him and he was planning on taking his family—he's got three or four girls you know—on a vacation. They were going to go, I think, to California, and now goddamit here I am at his rosary! "

"There's no way of knowing, compadre, one minute a man is on this earth and next it's vámonos a la chingada! " He snapped his fingers to emphasize the thin line between life and death.

"A man should always be ready to go . . ."

"Con huevos as they say, eh compadre."

They laughed and said it was true and each one wondered how he would meet his death. Would he greet him like a brother and take his hand and walk with him, or would he turn and spit in the face of death and tell him to go to his chingada madre. They didn't know, and that's why they reflected on the death of Sánchez because his death reminded them again that life wasn't worth anything, that it was only a mask to be worn for a brief time in that eternity that shrouded them.

The rosary ended and night fell like a mask over the barrio. The mourners filed out of the small mortuary chapel, offering the last condolences.

Across the street in the shadow of the elms Jason watched the widow and her daughters board a car and disappear into the heavy, green darkness of the night. When the street in front of the mortuary was empty Jason walked home. Throughout the night

31

the image of the dead man haunted his dreams, and also floating in the dreams was the face of the eldest daughter, the girl in mourning at the mortuary. Sometime during that restless night the girl removed her black mourning veil and when Jason saw her face he smiled and he could rest.

CHAPTER THREE

Each afternoon at five the shop whistle blew and released the men from work. The wail of steam carried as far as the darkest corner of Barelas where la India grubbed for roots and herbs along la Acequia, the deep irrigation canal that ran parallel to the river. There her mangy dogs returned the howl of the whistle and for a few seconds a strange dread filled the air. Mothers hushed their little children and told them to be good or else la Llorona would come and take them away. For a moment time stood still as the women prayed the day had ended well and the whistle was not signalling death. Then the sound died away and the brief tension eased away and children ran out to greet their fathers.

The soot-covered, weary men trudged down the street; their footsteps left somber marks on the dust of Barelas. A wildcat strike had been called to protest conditions at the shops and within the union itself. In retaliation the railroad fired the men and the company union rubber-stamped the act. The protesting workers found themselves without work and without the protection of their union. Coupled with that came a large lay-off. The angry men gathered at the union hall, only to find its doors closed to them. A spontaneous meeting was held at the nearby bar, and although there was a lot of talking and threats, after awhile the men accepted their defeat and grew sullen. They cursed the railroad and their own union leader who did not help them, then they walked home, dreading the thought of having to tell their families. For half the men of Barelas, hard times were coming with the summer's end.

Jason had filled a tub with water for his father, now he watched him as he scrubbed with soap then splashed it away with the clean water. He dried himself vigorously, like a young man, and Jason thought it was because of the dance that night.

"Are you going to the dance at the community center? " He asked.

"Yes, I think your mother wants to go," Clemente answered.

They were silent for awhile, then Jason asked, "How is work? "

Clemente looked at his son. There was something about his son that reminded him of himself when he was young. Sometimes he felt awkward when he talked with Jason, because he felt as if he was talking to himself. "Work is fine," he answered, "I'm lucky to have a job. They let some of the older men go. Today they fired Lalo, because he's been trying to organize the men so they can get rid of the union boss they have now—— Well, anyway it's none of my business. I stay clear of things like that, do my work and keep to myself. I don't understand their politics, so there's not much I can do to help——"

He paused and looked at the garden. Someone had already watered it and done some weeding so that the turned earth looked fresh.

"Anyway, perhaps the dance will raise the spirits of the community," he said.

"A wedding dance, for the daughter of the man who owns the supermarket——"

Clemente nodded. "His name is Mannie Garcia——"

"The vatos call him el Super," Jason laughed.

"Yes, I've heard his nickname," Clemente smiled. "Who are these vatos? " He asked. He was curious about his son's life. In the small town of Guadalupe he never worried about it, but here it seemed there was always some unknown danger out there, if only in the size and complexity of the city.

"Friends," Jason answered. "Chelo, Dickie, Pete, Pato, the cuates, and a crazy boy named Willie——"

"Are they pachucos? " Clemente asked.

"No——" Jason said while he emptied the gray, soapy water on the hard-packed ground by the steps.

Clemente felt relieved. "Well, this Mannie, el Super," he went on, "he must be some man. He started from nothing, I hear say, and now he's got the only supermarket in the barrio. He has a big Cadillac car, and a lot of political connections at City Hall. They say he delivers the barrio's votes every election, for the right price. Some of the people call him el patrón. Of course he takes his mordida from everyone—— Do you know he charges the people on welfare a dime to cash their checks. He gets a man a job, and he takes a bite. He gets someone out of jail, or helps someone apply for welfare or social security, and he gets a small cut. He charges a fee for everything, and all those small fees have made him rich——"

"It doesn't seem fair," Jason reflected.

"No," Clemente agreed, "but it's the way we're learning to live, like the americano, there is a fee for everything—— Hey, where's Benjie? "

"I think he's at the woodyard, the men are playing cards there——"

"Tell him to come home, it's time for supper." He watched Jason walk away then strutted into the kitchen. Adelita was at the stove; he moved quickly behind her and put his arms around her.

"Clemente——" She laughed. The warmth of his caress made her close her eyes. She felt her heart quicken.

"Like old times," he whispered.

"Yes," she answered, "like old times——" The strong embrace brought back old memories.

"I feel like a young man! " He laughed. "Tonight we will sing and dance all night! " He poured two glasses of wine and they toasted to their health. "Remember the night I met you, it was at a dance in Colonias, the night the Solís brothers killed my compadre Luis——"

"How can I forget," she smiled, "I thought my brothers would kill you that night because you danced and flirted with me all night, and you had not even asked my father's permission——" She paused. "I also remember the killing. I remember how cold it was that night. When we passed by and viewed the body, the blood was frozen on the ground. Why did they kill Luis? " she asked.

"It was a small thing, a thing of honor. He was drinking, and he spilled some wine on the new boots of Solís. Solís demanded an apology and my compadre refused. There were bad words exchanged, and so it became a thing of honor. They went outside, they were both armed——"

"It was a cold night," she shivered.

"Luis was a fool to go out alone; there were three brothers, so there is no telling what happened——"

"One of the secrets the llano keeps, shrouded by the snow of winter, washed away by the rains of summer——" she thought aloud.

"Yes," he nodded. "Where are the girls? "

"They have been in the bedroom all afternoon, arguing over a dress I bought for them—— There was only enough money for one dress, now they cannot decide who will wear it to the dance."

When they were all seated at supper he said, "It is not right for brothers and sisters to argue," and then to try to ease the tension he sensed between his daughters he told a story. It was a story that had been handed down for many generations, and it told about the evil that befell a disobedient daughter.

"——Her mother pleaded with the daughter not to go to the dance that night; she had had a premonition that something evil would happen. The daughter laughed at her mother and told her she was a superstitious old fool, and without permission she went off to the dance. There she met a young man, a stranger who swept her off her feet and danced with her the entire evening. She was envied by every other woman at the dance because the handsome stranger had eyes only for her, and she enjoyed the flirtations and the attention of the man as she never had before. She laughed as she thought how much she would have missed if she had heeded her mother's silly wishes.

"The handsome, young man waltzed so smoothly he seemed to glide, and when he spoke his soft words confused her thoughts and she promised herself to him. He was dressed in a dark, silk suit, and on his hands he wore soft, white gloves. She teased him about his gloves and asked him why he did not remove them, and he smiled and assured her that at midnight he would remove his gloves for her. For that she promised him the midnight dance, and so they laughed and danced and drank the stranger's sweet wine until the clock struck twelve. She stopped in the middle of the dance floor and announced to all that the stranger had promised to remove his gloves, and that when he had done so they would lead the midnight dance. Everyone watched and waited as the young man stripped away his beautiful white gloves. When he had done so the crowd cried in horror because the stranger's hands were the hairy, cloven hooves of the devil!

"The disobedient daughter froze with terror, but the devil held her close and made her dance the devil's dance with him, reminding her that she had promised herself to him. No one had the power to help her, until her father, who had watched all night at the window, broke through the fearful crowd and confronted the devil. 'En el nombre del Padre, del Hijo, y del Espíritu Santo! ' He invoked the name of the Holy Trinity and made the sign of the cross. Not even the devil himself can stand against the names of the Trinity and the sign of the holy cross! At the sound of the holy names he disappeared in a cloud of smoke!

"But the damage was already done. Even as the stench of sulfurous smoke consumed the devil, the young girl's features changed before their eyes. A coarse, gray animal hair grew all over her body, and she could no longer speak but only make growling sounds. She ran away and wandered alone in the llano for many years, crying for the soul she had lost, until she disappeared——"

Clemente finished the story and looked at his family. They had stopped eating while he told the story and now they sat very still. He hoped the message in the story would help calm the bad feelings between his daughters.

"Bah! " Juanita broke the silence, "I've heard that story before! And besides, things like that don't happen anymore! Anyway, I am older and I should wear the dress tonight! "

"She bought it for me! " Ana cried back.

"She bought it with my money! " Juanita slammed her fist on the table. "I'm the one that's working, and that gives me the right to——"

"Well I'm going to work too! " Ana jumped up. "I'm not going back to school! I'll get a job and have money and come and go as I want! "

"And where are you going to work? " Juanita sneered, "For las Golondrinas——"

"Juanita! " Clemente commanded, "¡Respeto a tus padres! "

And because she could find nothing else to say she shouted in

37

his face, "And don't call me Juanita! I hate that name! Call me Jan! All my friends call me Jan——"

He struck out and slapped her. The blow sent her reeling. "Your friends! " He shouted. "You mean those pachucos and marijuanos you spend your time with! " He trembled with rage. How could she deny her name? It had been his mother's name!

"Clemente! " Adelita gasped, "You have never before struck one of your children! " She reached out to comfort her daughter, but Juanita pushed her away.

"It didn't hurt! " She spat defiantly and dared her father to strike again. For a few agonizing moments they glared at each other, and in that time she demanded her freedom and dignity, and he understood that he was losing his command over her.

"Juanita, no! " Adelita exclaimed.

But Juanita challenged him again. "It's about time I had something to say about the way things are run around here! I work too! I have my own money! So I will come and go as I want, and nobody will rule me! " She dared everyone with her glare and when her challenge was not disputed she marched triumphantly from the room.

"Válgame Dios," Adelita groaned. "What is happening to us? " She asked her husband in disbelief.

Clemente sank into his chair. "I don't know," he shook his head, "I don't know——" He reached for the bottle of wine and drank. "She has always been Juanita," he muttered, "and now she wants to be Jan, like the americanos—Why? "

"Because it's old fashioned," Ana spoke up.

"Wha——" Clemente looked at his youngest daughter. Would she too defy him? He glanced nervously at Jason. It hurt him that his son should see his manhood stripped away, that he should see the man of the house lose his position.

"The people where Jan works say Wan-needa," Ana added, "so it's easier if they just say Jan——"

"Let them learn to pronounce it! " He cried out as if in pain. He felt his strength slipping away from him, but he didn't know how to recover it. "Leave me! Leave me! " He shouted in frustration, and when they were gone he sat in the evening darkness and drank. He cursed the day he had set foot in the city, and he cursed the time that was drawing his beautiful daughters out of his realm. There had to be a reason for the dissolution he felt around him, and as he drank and thought the only person he could find to blame was his wife.

Already he could hear Adelita in the bedroom, laughing with his daughters, settling the matter among themselves and pretending nothing had happened at the supper table. His command had not been heeded, and he was not needed to arbitrate this family matter. Even his sons no longer seemed to ask him for direction.

"Clemente! " Adelita called excitedly when they emerged from the bedroom, "Look! Everything is taken care off—— They could not decide who would wear the dress, and so they insisted that I should! " She was radiant with happiness. She looked as young as her daughters.

"It looks beautiful on you, mamá! " They cried and ran to hug and kiss her.

"Come," Adelita took her husband's arm, "Take us to the dance! "

His wife was like a young girl. She laughed and teased his dark mood away.

"Ah, what a beautiful night! " She exclaimed and took a deep breath of the night air. "It is just like the old times, Clemente! "

He nodded in agreement, but inside he felt that it was not so. He wondered where she had found the enthusiasm to challenge everything. He used to lead, and now he felt he didn't even know the road ahead of him while she nimbly and surely led the way up Barelas Street. The light was dim and he stumbled on the ruts of the road while she seemed to glide over the dark, uneven path.

"Don't worry about the girls," she tried to coax him out of his silence, "they will be all right. They are just growing up, and getting used to this new way of life. Things here are not as they were——"

The grillos in the dark elm trees picked up her refrain and their cricket-cry sang the melody that is eternal; and the thousand tongues of the trees swaying in the green night breeze whispered back that things are never quite what they were.

Clemente heard the song and he cried out, "But what will become of my familia! What will become of my land, of my roots——"

"Let it change," Adelita said. "We will make ourselves strong for the change that comes. If our roots and our crianza are deep enough, we have nothing to fear——"

"The music! " Juanita called up ahead. They had heard the music of the wedding dance and they were running.

"And the lights! " Adelita cried joyfully. The community center was brightly lit.

" ¡Entren! ¡Entren! " Mannie greeted everyone at the door, "La marcha is about to begin! " He was very happy, not only for his daughter who was marrying a gringo from the rich Country Club district, but for himself because of the business and political connections the marriage reflected. "Begin the wedding march! " He shouted, and feeble don Cristóbal took old doña Agapita's hand and began the promenade. Smart as a rooster he led the men's line and the women followed her. Up and down the hall they led the winding lines through the intricate steps of la marcha, their gaiety and rhythm setting a tone to the dance. As old and feeble as don Cristóbal was, and as much as her rheumatism bothered doña Agapita, they still controlled the lively, flirting lines with style and elegance.

After la marcha the men danced with the young bride, and each dance cost them a dollar bill which they pinned to the bride's dress. The women danced with the groom, and after that the dance began in earnest. Old compadres and old friends met to drink and laugh and talk. Sometime during the evening the bride was stolen by a group of men, and the groom was challenged to go and find his wife.

The old men of the barrio stood against the wall and watched the proceedings.

"Se robaron a la novia," one of them commented. They looked intently at the groom. What would he do?

"If he does not hurry," one of them winked his eyes and whispered to the rest of the chorus, "he might not find a virgin in his bed tonight——" They laughed.

"What can you expect," another added, "he is americano! " They roared with laughter and looked at the young groom who did not seem to know what was happening.

The dance continued, laughter flowed like sweet wine, los abrazos were exchanged freely. The pious talk of las viejitas mixed into the giggles of the young girls. The children who had earlier

40

shared in the merriment now fell asleep in the arms of a mother, a sister, una tía or an abuelita, anyone. They were all one family. The hours of the summer night tripped like drunkards into the time of eternity.

Outside the dance hall los vatos locos mounted those hours on the thin wings of marijuana smoke, and they too tripped into another sense of time. But the journey cost, and so the vatos who dispensed the barrio junk came to collect on their ticket.

"Hey," Chelo tapped Jason, "there's trouble outside! Some of the vatos from Sanjo are after your carnal."

"Benjie? " Jason asked, "Why? "

"He sold some junk for them, now they're here to collect and he doesn't have the money——"

Jason rushed outside. "Over by the gym! " Chelo pointed. They pushed past the vatos that had gathered to watch. Frankie, a pachuco Jason recognized, was shaking Benjie like a rag doll. Frankie was thick and squat, like a gorilla, and he was strong and mean; but that didn't bother Benjie. He was high on mota and he only laughed at Frankie's threat.

"You goin' pay us, ése, one way or another, you goin' to pay us! "

"Yeah! " His thin, weasel-faced friend hissed, "Wha'chu think the stuff was, free candy? " He pushed the button and the knife clicked open. He slashed out and the crowd of boys drew back.

"He's got a knife! " One of them shouted a warning.

Jason didn't hold back. He reached out, grabbed the hand that held the knife and jerked. Then he smashed his fist into the thin, bony face.

"Chingasos! Chingasos! " Someone shouted. "He got Flaco! " The rest of the gang that had been hanging around the dance hall came running, ready to jump in if it involved one of their own.

" ¡Jodido! " Frankie cursed as he saw his camarada go down. He reached out and grabbed Jason. He had thought the kid would be soft, like Benjie, so he wasn't ready for the explosive whallop that slammed a knee into his groin.

"Hijo 'ela chingada——" He doubled over in pain.

" ¡Cabrón! " Flaco cried and searched desperately for his knife. His nose and mouth were spurting blood and he cursed and swore he was going to kill Jason, but when he recovered his knife and

41

turned to face him the Barelas boys moved in to help Jason, and behind the group the men who had seen the fight were rushing towards them.

"Truchas! " Frankie shouted. He too had seen the men.

"Okay, okay," Flaco wiped his bleeding mouth, "we'll get you later, 'squadro ... you too, Benjie! " They turned and disappeared into the darkness.

The vatos cheered and shouted dirty names. Willie threw them fingers. It was the first time someone from Barelas had stood up to the two pachucos from Sanjo, and it had added meaning because Jason had done it for his brother.

"All right! " Willie slapped his hands, "he did it for his carnal! Okay, big daddy! " He hugged Jason.

"Damn, he got 'em both! He's a mean mutha! "

"It's about time someone took on those two marijuanos . . . but I'm glad it wasn't me——"

They pressed around Jason, praising him for what he had just done, but Jason was more concerned with getting Benjie away from the growing crowd of men.

"He's really high! " Chelo said.

"Help me get him out'a here—" Jason cried, and they put their arms around him to drag him away but it was too late. Clemente was one of the men who had come to break up the fight. When he saw Jason and Benjie he hurried forward.

" ¡Jasón! ¿Qué pasa? ¿Qué pasa? " he shouted.

"It's nothing, papá," Jason tried to reassure him, "Benjie had a couple of beers, but he's okay, we'll take him home——"

"There was a fight," one of the men told Clemente.

"A fight? But why? " Clemente asked. He reached out and grabbed Benjie.

"Those marijuanos, they were with your boy! " El Super charged through the crowd, a policeman in tow, "You better get him outta here! I don't want any marijuana here! Just good honest drinking, you hear! "

Clemente couldn't believe what he was hearing, but when he looked in Benjie's eyes he knew it was true. Benjie was mumbling and laughing incoherently.

"Benjamín! " Clemente moaned, "Oh my God, what has happened?"

"It's that crazy weed——" a man nodded.

"It's all right, papá, I'll take him home. Chelo will help, it's okay——"

They tried to pull Benjie away but Clemente stopped them. He knew what he had to do. In just a few weeks he felt his son had strayed away from him; he had given him too much freedom and in this strange city he had strayed. It was his duty to bring his son back into the circle of the family. He picked Benjie up, tossed him on his shoulder and walked away from the men. He carried him home and in the small shed behind the house he stripped the shirt off his son and beat him with an old leather strap. He had never beaten his children, but now in his frustration it was the only contact he knew to make with his son.

The sharp blows sobered Benjie. He raised his arm to protect himself and cried, "No more, papá! No more! " And when Clemente saw how cruel his blows had been he cursed and threw away the whip. He stumbled out of the shack, trembling from the rage and fear he felt, and ashamed of himself for what he had done. In the shed he heard Benjie groan and curse, and Clemente understood that a cleavage had come between father and son. He cursed the city and blamed himself for ever having come to it.

CHAPTER FOUR

Saturday afternoon, and they looped basketballs through the goal as easily as they would later confess their sins in the church across the street. Glistening with sweat and panting like dogs in a hot, summer day, they paused to rest on the cool strip of grass that bordered Coronado School.

"What are the cuates doing? " Jason asked. The cuates were the twins, a part of the gang Jason had found with Chelo, Pato, Pete, Dickie, and crazy Willie.

"They're talking about a midnight trip to las Golondrinas," Dickie answered.

"You mean the women who have the shack down by the ditch, and——"

"Yeah! " Willie laughed crazily. He rolled on the grass and exploded with energy. "Ha, haugh, hough, ugh, ugh! " He grunted.

"Careful, Willie, you wanna save some for las Golondrinas, if we go——"

"Willie's gonna have to go see them sometime, he's still a virgin! " The gang laughed, and Willie could only answer, "Ooooooh-sí, a virgin! "

"It's true, Willie, the best thing you ever had was a wet dream! " They laughed again.

"We're ready! " The cuates shouted. They came around the lilac bushes.

"Ready for what? "

"Ready for confession," they said seriously and pointed across the street at the church.

"They confess their sins ahead of time," Dickie explained to Jason, "That way they can go prowling tonight and raise hell and still come to mass tomorrow and go to communion."

"It's something the whole world does," Willie said, "Have it now, pay later; confess now, sin later—— just stay ahead of the collector."

"Come on, Willie, quit messing up the grass! " Pato complained. To get even and annoy Willie he farted in Willie's direction and shouted, "Catch that and paint it red! "

"Oooooh-sí, red——"

"Anyway," Dickie went on, "the cuates are the lovers of the barrio. They keep the country club girls happy—— them and Pato."

"Pato got the Japanese girl whose parents have the candy store on Third Street, right Pato? "

Pato grinned. "Well, whenever you want advice on how to make it, let a real man tell you," he beamed and pointed a thumb at his chest.

"Hey, Pato, is it true they have it sideways? " Pete asked.

Pato looked disturbed for a moment, then he quickly composed himself and nodded, "Yeah, as a matter of fact she did have it sideways——" Just like the rumor, he thought, and grinned.

"You lie like a mutha! " Willie laughed, "I saw the whole family at Tingley Beach last summer, and they went behind the bushes to dress, and I watched, and the girls don't have it sideways! "

" ¡Me la rayo por mi jefita! " Pato swore, and then he quickly changed the subject and started talking about the car he was going to get as soon as school started.

"Let's quit bullshitting," Willie said, "most of us ain't ever gotten any——"

"How about you, Jason? "

"No."

"At least he's honest about it! "

"Well, we tried," Dickie said lamely. "We heard there was this place on South Broadway, so we got drunk one night last summer, and we went down there——"

"There were mostly blacks there," Pato added. "Crazy Willie got drunk on wine and he went around shouting poontang! Poontang! "

"And suddenly this door opens and this big, black sonofabitch comes out and grabs Willie! "

"Yeah," Willie's eyes rolled wildly as he remembered, "he lifted me up by the collar and he took me in this room where there were three black women and one white woman, and they had almost nothing on, and they were sitting around smoking and drinking beer and listening to Leadbelly blues. And that cabrón, he took me up to one of them and he rubbed my face all over her boobies! Man, I thought I was gonna shit! "

"And then he threw Willie out and he told him if he ever came back he was goin' to rub his face somewhere else! " They rolled on the grass and laughed as they remembered.

"Anyway, we never went back——" Pato said.

"Besides," Chelo added, "you're supposed to wait till you get married——"

"Nah, man, wha'da you mean! " Pato exclaimed, "And miss out on all the fun! "

"I'm just repeating what the priest said——"

"Ah, what does the padrecito know! " Willie made a sour face. "Padre Cayo is a chispa himself, I bet he's gotten his! "

"Yeah, I'm gonna get as much as I can before I get married," Dickie agreed with Pato.

"It's a sin," Chelo insisted.

"You're crazy! And so what if it is, all you gotta do is go to confession, like the cuates——"

"That's right," the cuates nodded, "ten Hail Marys for penance and you got a clean record, ready to go again! "

"Well, let's look at it this way," Willie said, "suppose it's not a sin, but if you're goin' to screw around before you get married, doesn't the woman you're going to marry have the same right too? "

"Hey! Wait a minute, wha'chu saying? What kind of a stupid question is that! "

"Don't listen to Willie, he's pendejo! Bien tapado——"

"All I said is if you do it, she can do it," Willie grinned.

"Chale! Hell no! " Pato protested vigorously.

"I expect the girl I marry to be a virgin! " Dickie said emphatically.

"Damn right! " Pete agreed. "It's all right for the man to screw around, but not the woman. That's the way it's always been! "

"That's right," they all agreed. "And that's the way it should

46

stay——"

"Yeah, Willie, and if you think differently you're goin' go queer——"

"You're crazy even to think that way, Willie. You start thinking like that and changing the way it's always been and everything will get messed up. My old man says, keep the women home and keep them busy with children, and they're happy. Why man, in my family there ain't ever been any divorce! "

"Yeah, it's women that run around that get divorced! "

"Okay! Okay! " Willie laughed. "Look at it this way. Suppose she did it, and you didn't find out until after you had married her? "

"I'd kill her! " Pato threatened. "¡Toma! ¡Un chingaso! " And in his mind he saw the viper of his manhood strike out and destroy his unfaithful woman.

"You can never be sure——" Pete sighed.

"Damn! How can they be like that? " Dickie added.

"I'll never marry," Pato said somberly. He spit out the grass with which he had been picking his teeth and repeated, "I swear I'll never marry! "

"Me neither," Dickie agreed.

"Let's make a promise; we'll never marry! "

" ¡Orale! " " ¡A toda madre! " " ¡Por Dios Santo! " They all agreed.

"Let's cut our wrists and as blood brothers seal our promise! " Willie said, describing the way he'd seen it in the movies.

"No, pendejo, we don't have to cut our wrists," Pato hesitated at the suggestion, "let's just shake hands on it! "

"Okay, and the first one to break the promise won't get a cherry wife," Dickie added. They paused and looked at each other. They couldn't back down in front of the group, and so like men, they shook hands. All except the cuates, who said they didn't expect their wives to be cherry anyway.

"That's the problem with women nowdays, they don't have any respect—— In the old days it was a thing of honor. Hell, you found your old lady fooling around and you let her have it! "

"Orale, I feel like getting even with all of them! "

"Let's go up to Broadway and get some," Pato suggested.

"Yeah! " Dickie agreed. "Hell, it's the end of summer, and we

47

should so something big before school starts! "

"Nah, but that black cat up there knows us——"

"Well, how about a visit to las Golondrinas? "

"Are you kidding, man? Have you seen them? They're big and fat! I mean really big! They've got hips as wide as the church door, titties bigger than watermelons——"

"They'd swallow you up, like getting lost in a big cave——"

"They're like mountains, too big to grab ahold of, too big to enter——" They thought about the immense task of mounting one of the Golondrina sisters and they hesitated.

"Well, are we gonna talk or are we gonna do it? " Pato asked. The image of the naked mountain of flesh had moved him past his doubt.

"——Do it," Dickie nodded.

"Orale, we'll all go! " They agreed. In the strength of the group each one found his own nerve. Suddenly the excitement of their manhood flowed through their blood and made them cry out like a herd of hot, excited goats. They were ready to embark upon that adventure that sealed their manhood. They shook hands all around, and they slapped each other on the back and said they'd get some wine and be real men.

"Not me" Chelo said, and he casually stood up. He looked towards the western horizon where the setting sun had painted a flashing red backdrop. In a moment the color would disappear and the scene would be in darkness. He wondered if he was afraid to go, or if he didn't go because he truly believed in the rules of the old priest whom he saw opening the doors of the church.

"Hey! Where you goin', Chelo? "

"Confession," he called back, and the ringing of the church bell which gathered the old women of the barrio drowned his words.

" ¡Santuchas! " Pato called after him, " ¡Pirujo! "

"Ah, let him go, there's still enough of us left——"

"I don't know," Willie vacillated.

"You gonna back down too, Willie? Damn, and I thought you were the big cabrón! " Pato shook his head. "Come on, man, don't be nalgas! We'll get some wine, it'll be all right, you'll see——"

"I'm not backing down," Willie said, "I was just thinking—— It's getting dark, and I was thinking about the old witch who lives near

48

las Golondrinas——" He shivered.

"What about her? "

Willie shrugged. "Some say she's la Llorona——"

"Come on! " Dickie said sarcastically, "There ain't no such thing as la Llorona! "

"Can you imagine la Llorona in the barrio," Pete said cynically, "the cops would bust her ass! That pinche ley doesn't understand any of that stuff; as far as they're concerned la Llorona would be one more tecato crying from withdrawal pains! "

"Los vatos locos, the real crazy vatos on the street say there's only one Llorona now," Dickie added, "and that's the siren of a cop's car. That mother friggin' ley comes blaring down the street, busting heads, throwing the vatos in the can, and they rot there, they die there——"

"Maybe so," Willie said, "It's funny how things aren't like they used to be. It used to be la Llorona was a ghost, a shadow, a cry one heard in the brush of the river or near la 'cequia. Now it's becoming more and more real, now it's the cop's siren, now we can see it, we actually see it eating up the men of the barrio——"

"The men of the shops call the whistle la Llorona," Pete added.

"Yeah, that's what I mean," Willie nodded, "and we can see that Llorona too, and it destroys more people in one day than any of the old Lloronas ever did—— What was la Llorona? A part of a story, a shadow, and we were just a little afraid of her then; she seemed to be a part of our lives—— Now, now they're out in the open, they're real monsters! "

They agreed. They thought of all the stories they had heard about the wailing demon-woman looking for her lost son, and they knew that what crazy Willie said made sense.

"Yeah, but are we going or not? " Pato asked and brought them back to reality.

"She's got la piedra mala," Willie whispered.

"Bullshit! "

"What is it? "

"It's a black rock . . . they say she brought it up from Mexico . . ."

"What does it do? "

"You sell your soul to the devil and the black rock brings you money, money and women——"

49

"Hey, cool! That's what we want! "

"Hey, don't bullshit with that stuff, ése. My ole man saw that rock, and he said he threw up just seeing it . . . then to get the money or the women you have to touch it, and they say it's alive, it's like acid . . ."

"Damn, sounds scary," one of the cuates whistled in the dark.

"I'd do anything for a piece, but not mess around with that black rock . . ."

"Some people hear singing when they touch it, some can speak to it and it answers . . ."

"A woman saw her son killed in Korea——"

"A man from Isleta found a buried treasure after he talked to the rock——"

"Bullshit! "

"Maybe so, but it's a strange thing, isn't it? Those rocks are a million years old, a jillion . . . they were here when the people arrived . . . the very first people who ever came . . ."

"The Indians? "

"Yeah . . ."

Suddenly the last of the light that had lingered in the clouds of the west disappeared, and the sky grew dark.

——*The gods of darkness that slept in the ancient volcanos rose and walked. Under the volcanos the earth groaned in its eternal sleep, in its eternal dream . . .*

"That piedra mala feeds on pins and needles," Willie whispered hoarsely. "They say the old witch lives only to forge the pins and needles for her rock. Bultos and ruidos haunt the house. My father, who is the only man to dare to walk in that dark corner of Barelas, has seen those strange shadows that haunt her hut, and he's heard the noises. The old woman can't sleep. She is cursed——"

Jason shivered. "I'd like to see that stone; I'd like to feel its power——"

"Impossible," Willie shook his head.

"Come on! " Pato complained, "You two are giving me the shivers! Let's quit talking about all that spooky stuff—— damn, Jason, you been hanging around Willie too long, you're beginning to talk like him. You better watch it, ése, word will get around that you're——" He waved his finger at his head.

50

"Crazy! " Dickie said. "Willie's whole family is like that. Willie's jefito feeds them dog meat! Rufus, Willie's dad, he goes aroun——" He was going to go on, but Jason said, " ¡Córtatelas! Cut it out, man! " And he looked Dickie straight in the eyes and Dickie backed down. It was the first time they felt Jason take a leadership position within the gang.

"Come on," one of the cuates said, "we've already missed confession and it's gotten dark. Let's go down to Ruppe's Drugstore and buy the rubbers and get the hell on with it! "

"I agree," Pato said and stood up. " ¡Vamos, raza! "

They walked down Fourth Street to the drugstore. They stopped at the Blue Moon Bar where Pato used a false id to buy some wine, and it didn't matter that he didn't fit the identification because Justo, the owner of the bar, sold to anyone. When they neared the drugstore they flipped a coin to see who would go in and buy the rubbers, and Willie lost.

"Shit! " He complained as they pushed him through the door. "I can't do it! " He turned and started to run, but Pato held him.

"Come on, Willie, you get firsts at las Golondrinas if you buy the rubbers! "

"It's against the law to buy them, ain't it? " Willie protested.

"Nah, tell them it's for your old man or something——"

"Well, what the hell do I ask for? " Willie cried helplessly as they pushed him towards the door, "I can't just go in there and ask for rubbers! "

They looked to the twins for help. "Tell him you want a package of Mereh-Willows," the cuates said, "'that's what they're called.

"Mer-eh-willows," Willie repeated the sound.

"Yeah, satisfaction guaranteed! " The cuates smiled and reassured him.

Willie took a deep breath and walked into the drugstore. He wandered up and down the aisles looking for anything that closely resembled a package of prophylactics, while the faces at the window watched. He wished for help, but the only other person in the store was the fat girl at the counter, and he was too embarassed to ask her. She was a big pachuca. Her eyes were dark with mascara, her eyebrows painted on, her lips bright red, and her hair was teased and fluffed out around her round face. On her

51

forehead was tattoed a small, blue cross, the mark of the pachuco. Her low-cut blouse exposed the better halves of two huge breasts which rested comfortably on the counter. She noticed Willie and looked up from her *True Confession* magazine.

"Hey, whadaya want, ése? " She shouted.

"Nah-nahthing! " Willie stammered.

"Whadaya mean, nahthing! " She repeated and walked towards him, swinging her big hips. She moved the wad of gum she had been chewing into her cheek and said, "You been lookin', ain'cha? "

Willie took a deep breath. "I want a package of Mer-eh-willows," he repeated the sounds exactly as he had heard them.

"Mer-eh-willows," the girl said. She scratched her head and thought. Finally she puckered her lips and shook her head. "Whas that? " She asked.

Oh shit, Willie thought, the first time I try to buy rubbers and I get a virgin. He felt the palms of his hands sweating.

"Mer-eh-willows——" he repeated, enunciating carefully.

"Well, whas it for? " She asked.

Willie swallowed hard. "It's for, well it's for, que chingao! It's for when you go to bed! Yeah, for when you go to bed! " He looked at her big melons and gave her the eye. She'd get the message!

"Ohhhhh," she smiled, "it's like pajamas or something, eh? "

Willie shook his head in frustration. "No, no, no—— You put them on like pajamas, but they're not pajamas——"

"Well, I don' know what it is," she shrugged. "Ruppe! " She called the pharmacist. Willie felt himself getting red.

"¿Qué pasa? " The old man came from the back room and looked at Willie.

"I don' know what this guy wants," she popped her gum, "he asked for Mer-eh-willows, but I don' know what that is——"

"Mer-eh-willows, eh? " The pharmacist stroked his chin. "Is someone sick? " He asked. He knew it wasn't an herb or a remedy; he had been selling to the barrio all his life and he knew them all. Perhaps it was a new medicine; there seemed to be a new one every day since the war, and he couldn't keep up with all of them.

"No, nobody sick——"

"Who in the family needs it? " The man asked.

"My father," Willie nodded, "yeah, my father! "

"For his stomach? "

"No."

"Maybe he has been drinking too much," the pharmacist said sympathetically, "¿está crudo? "

"No," Willie answered. He felt like turning and running.

"Well, where's he goin' to put it? " The girl asked in exasperation. "Whas it you do with Mer-eh-willows, eh? "

"Don't you know," Willie groaned, "don't you know that Mer-eh-willows are rubbers, and that they're used to screw! "

The old pharmacist and the girl looked at each other and burst out laughing. The old man laughed until he choked and cried. Willie thought he was going to have a heart attack. The girl's big breasts trembled like jell-o as she shook with laughter, and her mascara ran and spread down her fat cheeks.

"They're for you! " She cried through her laughter, "You're going to——"

"Mer-eh-willows! " The pharmacist cried between gasps for breath, and when he could laugh no more he reached behind the counter and handed Willie a small package of prophylactics.

Willie read the label. *Merry Widow. Dependable. Lasting power."*

"They're on me——" The old man wiped his tears of laughter. Willie turned and dashed out. Behind him he heard the man call, "Hey! Do you know where to put them! " And he elbowed the girl and their laughing fit began anew. Ripples of laughter followed Willie and rang in his ears until in the alley he took a long drink of Tokay wine.

They all drank and began their odyssey down the back streets of the barrio towards the whorehouse.

"Here we come! " They shouted. " ¡Chapete! "

They shouted only where they could not be heard, and they walked only in darkness so that they could not be seen moving down the river of their downfall. They were shadows, tripping down dark alleys toward the nest of the swallows. They were the boys of summer, windfall of grace and innocence, taking their sperm-rich boyhood to the swallow-thronged barn. They drank the wine of the summer sun and shouted into the darkness that they were men.

53

"¡Yo soy hombre!" "We are men! " "Golondrinas! You are going to feel a man like you never have before! "

They boasted and drank the wine that fanned the fire in their loins, and they shouted and slapped each other on the back to work up their resolution so that they would not feel the empty, gnawing fear in their stomachs.

"Golondrinas! " They called, "Here we come! Hulo-oooooo . . ." And the echo of their false bravado was lost in the entangled darkness. They knocked at the door of the fallen swallows and pushed their way into the beds of straw.

Oh, my God! They moaned at the sight of mountains of hot, quivering flesh. Red, cavernous lips nauseated them with kisses, and embraces smelling of sobaco drew them down. Breasts of rolling flesh cradled them, and rough hands pulled wet, wilted flowers to mate the pollen of the bush. My God! They screamed and turned to run——

"Our boys! Our boys! " The squealing sisters called.

They fell upon the whores, and realized that in the conquest of their ruined sisters they could find themselves.

"Aie! Aie! Aie-iiiiiiii——" Their gritos split the air.

" ¡A toda madre! "

" ¡Hijo 'ela chingada! A toda madre——"

" ¡Yo soy hombre! " They boasted, and having proved their manhood they slid off sweating thighs.

Las Golondrinas sung lullabies for their conquerors, but the new men turned away and felt a sickness gnaw within. The wine was gone. Only the emptiness remained. There wasn't much to talk about as they walked away. They took deep breaths of the cool night air and paused to light cigarettes. They hurled the empty wine bottles into the darkness. In the silence of the night the bottles crashed against gnarled cottonwood trees which, like old grandfathers, shuddered at the painful growth of boys, the boys of summer who wound their way towards winter gray.

CHAPTER FIVE

Right before school started Cindy had a party. They were sitting around the Red Ball Cafe one night, drinking cokes, killing time and bragging when Pato came running in.

"Crazy! Crazy! Crazy! Vatos! Get your dancing calcos on, Cindy's having a party tonight! And I just got us an invite! "

"You lie like a mutha! " Willie said.

"Since when has Cindy invited any vatos locos to her pad? " Pete asked.

"Since she saw Jason at Tingley Beach, that's since when! " Pato beamed and hugged Jason. "Ah my little country boy from Guadulupe, Cindy's got the hots for you, and that means we're going over to her cool place and drink her old man's booze and screw all the gabachitas from the Country Club! Ummmm, I love you! " he pinched Jason's cheeks.

"Cut it out, Pato," Jason pushed him away. "Make sense. Who's Cindy? "

"You don't remember her! Hey man, you're blind! Or you don't like girls? Shame, shame . . . Cindy's the blonde we saw at Tingley Beach Saturday, remember? She's the one all the vatos were trying to score with. She lives there at the Country Club, oh man do they have a big place. Her old man's a lawyer or some-thing. And——"

"She's the number one cheerleader at la Washa," Willie broke in, "and there ain't a vato there that wouldn't give his left you-know-what just to go down once with her."

"She's a nice chick," Dickie said coolly, "she's really beautiful."

"So how come she's turned on Jason? " one of the cuates asked.

"Who cares! " Pato exclaimed. "He's a country boy, ain't he, so she likes country boys . . . none of these crazy vatos from the

55

barrio for her. Anyway, she asked me who he was Saturday, but I didn't pay any attention. I was busy trying to score myself. So today she asked me again and then she said if I would take him to the party tonight the rest of us were welcome——"

"All right! " they cheered. They believed Pato now and the excitement of late summer coursed through their veins. "Let's go! " they shouted and stomped out the cafe onto the hot, summer-night street.

"I could tell by the way she asked she's got the hots——" Pato continued. They razzed Jason.

"What's our boy got that we don't know! "

"Golondrina fever! "

They laughed and went swinging down the street, feeling good, feeling high on the prospects of the party. They crossed the broad belt of zoo and park that separated the barrio from the rich section of town that bordered the golf course. In the dark they heard strange animal sounds, grunts and shrieks and the shrill cries of birds.

"Damn spooky place," one of the cuates said nervously.

"Not as spooky as that place where the Golondrinas live. I ain't ever goin' back there——"

"No matter how hard up you get? "

They laughed nervously, clung together as a group, and crossed the park. The air was cool. Beyond the shadows of the giant alamos they could see the well-lighted streets of the Country Club district.

"Do you know where she lives? " Chelo asked.

"Yeah, yeah, last year she invited the basketball team for hamburgers, when we took city . . . You should see the place, it's big."

"Did you get anything besides hamburgers? "

Pato snickered. "Don't worry, there's plenty of little skinny Golondrinas running around here. You'll see——"

They followed the street to a large court and heard the music. The large, rambling ranch-style house was dimly lighted. It was set back and fronted by a wide lawn.

"We're here! " Pato called. He combed back his ducktail and rang the bell. A blonde girl opened the door and smiled.

"Hi, Pat, come on in! " She shouted above the strains of Fats

Domino's rock. They entered the dark hall. It was late and the party was already well under way. In the big front room twisting bodies jumped to the be-bop.

"You know the guys," Pato said.

"Yes, I guess I know them all from school," Cindy smiled. "Come on in, make yourselves at home——"

"And this is Jason," Pato introduced Jason.

Cindy held out her hand. "I'm Cindy," she said, and when she touched his hand Jason felt her warmth. He looked into her clear blue eyes and thought she was beautiful. "——I guess you'll be going to Washington when school starts——"

"Yes," he stammered and looked away. The vatos had disappeared, melted into the shadows that twisted on the dance floor.

"Come in," she said and drew him in, still holding his hand. "I'll introduce you to some of the kids . . . They all go to la Washa as we call it." She laughed and he followed her into the room. She introduced him to a few kids then asked him if he wanted something to drink. All the kids were drinking and from somewhere flowed the strong smell of marijuana smoke.

"A beer's fine——" he answered.

The kitchen was packed with boys. "Come on, everybody out on the dance floor! " Cindy called gaily, and the boys smiled and moved out to join the dancers. There was something about her voice and presence that called for respect. She handed him a beer and the drink settled the queasy feeling in his stomach.

"Where's your parents? " Jason asked.

"My father's on a business trip and mom went with him," Cindy answered. "Anyway, once a year they let me have a big party on my own, as long as I keep it cool it's okay——" she reassured him, and then she added, "and I've always kept it cool," and smiled. There was a moment of awkward silence which she broke by saying she had seen him at the Beach. He smiled and said he had seen her too, but he lied. He didn't remember her, and like the vatos he wondered why she had picked him.

"I knew you were new——" she said, and he told her a little about Guadalupe.

"Do you like it here? " she asked, and they spent his beer making small talk. "Do you dance? " she asked when the beer was gone. He tried to tell her he didn't but she wouldn't listen. She pulled him out on the dance floor and said she'd teach him. The be-bop step was simple, she coaxed and kidded him until he laughed and joined her. They let themselves go it felt good to jump to the rhythms of Bill Haley, Little Richard, Bo Diddley and all the rest. And when they slowed the tempo and he held her tightly in a slow waltz he wasn't asking himself anymore questions; he was enjoying her closeness and growing with an exhilaration he had never felt before. She felt the same and whispered in his ear, "I wanted to meet you . . . I'm glad I met you . . ."

From time to time she ran off to take care of little things that kept the party going and each time she smiled at him and told him not to go away that she would return. Willie appeared during one of the breaks.

"Damn this place is big! " he muttered. "Did you see the swimming pool out back? They don't have to go swimming in la'cequia like we do, huh? A bunch of them are swimming back there and daring the girls to go nude. ¡Chingao! "

"Where's the rest of the vatos? " Jason asked.

"Ah, they're spread around . . . Pato's doing a snow job on two little gabachitas back there, I don't know where the rest are . . ."

Chelo showed up. "Hey, how's it going? "

"All right, all right," Willie wiped at his nose, "free booze and food, it's all right! "

"Maybe it's time to split," Chelo said nervously.

"What's the matter, man, you can't find a chick! " Willie laughed.

"No, but you'd never guess who showed up——"

"Captain Marvel, Superman, Tarzan, Buck Rogers, Tin Tan——"

"Cool it Willie," Chelo looked around the crowd nervously, "Sapo's here——"

Willie cooled it. "Goddamn, Sapo! It is time to leave! How in the hell did he get invited? "

"He came with Cristina. She knows Cindy pretty well, and I guess she got invited——"

"Who in the hell's Sapo? " Jason asked.

"Sapo's a big chuco, ah, he's a cool guy but he's crazy. He just got out of reforma, the Springer reformatory——"

"For? "

"He did time for killing a guy during the Sanjo and Barelas pachuco fights . . . he doesn't like vatos from Barelas . . ."

"So what does that have to do with us? Why should we leave because he doesn't like anyone from Barelas? " Jason shook his head and smiled.

"Nah, you don't get it, ése, Sapo is a real friend of Flaco and Frankie . . . I mean they're a gang and now that Sapo's back he's the leader again, and when he finds out what you did to them he's going to come after you, and us . . ."

"He already knows," Chelo said, "he asked me who Jason was——"

"Where is he? " Jason asked above the blaring music. Chelo searched and pointed across the room at a tall, well built chuco. Sapo wore a full ducktail like Pato's, and although his complexion was sallow and his face thin, he had a soft handsomeness that attracted the girls. They surrounded him by the light near the record player. They were laughing at something he had said.

"He looks pretty regular," Jason shrugged, but he was no longer looking at Sapo. His attention was riveted on the girl who stood by him. It was the girl Jason had seen at the mortuary, Sánchez's daughter, the same smooth face that had haunted his dreams since the night he saw her.

"——No, no," Willie was pulling at him, "you don't understand. Sapo's cool, but when he starts shooting junk he goes crazy, and it won't be long before he's shooting! Look, let's just get the hell outta here. It's been a nice party, so why spoil it——"

But it was too late; Jason was walking across the room, pushing his way past the dancers toward Sapo. All Chelo and Willie could do was follow.

Sapo had sensed he was being watched, now he turned and faced Jason. His dark eyes narrowed as he studied the kid who had gotten the best of Flaco and Frankie, then his full lips parted in a smile. So the kid was coming to meet him, well at least he had guts. But huevos weren't going to be enough, Sapo thought, because sooner or later he was going to have to bust the square's head, yeah he was going to have to do it just to prove to Flaco and the rest that he could still run the gang. He slipped his hand under the one-button jacket and felt the zip gun he had made in reform school, and he felt easier, but he wished he was high because when

59

he was high his blood didn't feel so cold and the excitement of the galloping rush allowed him to do things without thinking.

"Jason! " Cindy reached Jason just as he approached Sapo, "Let's dance."

"I was going to say hello——" Jason nodded at Cristina.

"Oh, you know Cristina? " Cindy asked, and a small frown crossed her face.

"No, I——"

"Come on, I'll introduce you," Cindy smiled and pressed close to him and whispered, "her father was killed this summer, in an accident . . . I think it's the first time she's been out so everybody's being cool——Cristina, this is Jason . . ." And Cristina turned and smiled at Jason.

"Hi, I've heard a lot about you——"

"And I don't know your friend's name," Cindy turned to Sapo.

"Oh that's okay, baby," Sapo grinned, "your friend knows my name——" They looked at each other. "Yeah, he knows my name, and he knows my friends . . . right 'squadro? " He laughed softly and Jason felt the bad blood in him, and he knew Willie was right, sooner or later Sapo was going to come after him.

Cindy also felt the tension. She looked nervously at Cristina and said, "Look, I don't want any trouble——"

Cristina looked at Jason and then at Sapo. "No, there won't be any trouble . . . we were just leaving. Thanks for inviting me, but I could only come for a little while, and Lawrence, well he just got back, and he offered to bring me. But I really have to go . . ." She pulled Sapo away.

"Yeah, it's really nice to see people again," Sapo laughed. He brushed Jason as he went by. "See you around, square." The dancers parted to let them pass. They knew about Sapo and nobody wanted to mess with him.

"Damn! " Willie exclaimed, "Why did you wanna come and meet him for! He's gonna think you're pushing him . . ."

They didn't know that it wasn't Sapo he wanted to meet but Cristina, and that it was she that he looked after as they left.

"Come on, let's dance," Cindy said and pulled him out to the middle of the room, but it didn't matter how close she held him or how many beers he drank he couldn't erase the image of Cristina floating before his eyes. When Willie and Chelo left Jason was ready to go with them but Cindy begged him to stay. Pato and the cuates had disappeared long ago, and Pete and Dickie had gone with Nick to another party.

"Don't go," she kept saying, "everybody's almost gone——" She took him out to the patio where it was cool and then she went inside and pulled the plug on the record player and announced the party was over. She returned to sit by him. "Everybody's gone," she said, and in the dark her voice was soft. "Did you enjoy it? " she asked and moved into· his arms. Her breath was warm and sweet on his face.

"Yes, it was great," he nodded, and still he was filled with a restlessness that called him away. Her soft lips pressed against his and they sank into the lush grass. For a moment he returned her kiss and embrace as the pounding of his heart erased everything. Then he pulled away suddenly and said, "I have to go . . ."

"Jason, don't go," she pleaded. "I, I've never asked anyone to stay before——" she added.

"I know—— It's not that," he answered. He looked beyond the fence to the dark green outline of the alamos of the park. Beyond that lay Barelas. He felt uneasy because he didn't want to stay and make love to Cindy, then he thought he heard the faint melody of a guitar and he smiled. "I've got to go," he said simply, and without looking back he started across the lawn.

"Jason! Please don't go! " He heard Cindy call behind him. "Jason! "

He leaped the cinder block fence and headed home. Around him the midnight shadows of the night shut out the moon, and for awhile the heavy smell of the zoo animals and their strange noises surrounded him. Then he broke past the dark curtain and saw ahead of him the warm lights of the barrio.

CHAPTER SIX

It was the last Sunday of summer and after mass the people of Barelas gathered at the park. Men took pride in walking the paseo with their families and took time to visit with old neighbors. Old friends from the different barrios of the city met and the nexus was kept intact as the different barrios formed one larger community.

"Every barrio is my barrio," old Manual liked to say. "In the old days it used to be las colonias, the ranchitos, the pueblos, and whenever we traveled from one to the other we were always welcomed. It was the way of the people. This is the way it should be . . ."

So women prepared picnic lunches, the barrio feuds were set aside and the energy of the young men was dissipated in baseball games, and the men washed their cars and kept a close watch on their daughters who gathered in groups to walk in the park. The pachucos rode low in their cars, feeling cool and looking over the girls, always watching for a movida. There was peace as the people came from Old Town, Duranes, Martineztown, San Jose, Williams, South Broadway, Sawmill and from as far away as Armijo, Atrisco, Griegos, and Alameda to enjoy the last Sunday of summer in the coolness of the park.

Jason was also on his way to the park to meet the vatos. He had just crossed a thicket of tall lilac bushes when he saw Willie running towards him. He was shouting for Jason to stop.

"Hey, ¿qué pasa? " Jason asked.

Willie skidded to a stop. He stood panting in front of Jason and wiped at his nose. "Haven't you heard? " he asked as he tried to tuck in his oversized shirt.

"Heard what? "

"The word's out on the street, Flaco and Frankie are out to get you! Today! And Sapo's with them; they just left the Red Ball, higher than hell, an——"

"Hey, slow down Willie," Jason smiled. "What's the problem? "

Willie pulled at his pants. "The problem is those crazy tecatos are after you! " Willie shouted.

"Come on, man, you know I'm not afraid of those grifos——" Jason put his arm on Willie's shoulder and tried to calm him. "And you know they're not going to try anything, not with the vatos around . . ."

"Ah, Jason, you can't count on the vatos! When the rumble starts it's every mutha for himself! They'll run from Sapo——" He realized what he had said and added, "I won't run, Jason, even though I'm afraid of that crazy Sapo and his gun, I'll back you up . . . and so will Chelo . . ."

"So there's three of us," Jason smiled. "Come on, take it easy; let's go play ball. Where'd the rumble talk start? " he asked as they walked along the hedge.

"There's always a rumble on the last day of summer . . . Man, the barrios go at each other and all hell breaks loose! "

"Ah, come on, Willie, it'll probably only involve a few vatos who want to make like big machos . . . Come on or we'll miss the ballgame——"

"Nah," Willie hesitated, "let's skip that today. Let's go over to my house and you can meet my brother Henry . . . I never invited anyone over to my house before." He paused and looked at Jason. "Cause of what they say, you know, that my old man's a dog killer, and that we're all crazy . . . You're the only one that don't say that . . ."

"Well you're not, Willie," Jason smiled and put his arm around his friend. "The vatos only say that to get you mad. You can't believe in what people say, you gotta believe in yourself. Now let's go play ball——"

Willie shook his head. "I'm afraid," he said. "Sapo's with them and the word's out on the street that he's carrying a zip gun and that he's all crazy on junk. He's saying he's gonna get you for what you did to Flaco and Frankie, he's gotta prove himself . . . I've seen that guy when he's crazy, he goes wild . . ." He turned and pointed at the car that had suddenly roared up the street and blocked them. "Damn! It's too late! " he shouted.

63

Sapo, Flaco and Frankie came bounding out of the car and backed them up against the tall bushes. They came at Jason and Willie slowly, smiling, taking their time. Frankie was swinging a bike chain. Flaco held a push-button knife.

"So how's it goin', 'squadro? " Sapo grinned. Jason looked at his wild eyes and sensed what Willie meant. This wasn't the same cool vato he had met at the party. Sapo's face was contorted and his voice was cold and cruel. "I heard you messed with my camaradas," Sapo hissed, "so we came to even the score. Nobody's ever goin' to touch any of Sapo's friends and get away with it, understand. So we're goin' make a lesson outta you . . . Flaco, you take the pendijito! " He pushed Flaco towards Willie.

They squared off, moving slowly towards each other, tensing for the blows that would come, at the same time moving Jason and Willie back against the bushes so they couldn't break through. Jason and Willie were ready to fight, until Sapo pulled his zip.

He laughed wildly. "Hey man! Ever see one of these before? It blows a big hole in you! " He laughed as they pressed forward.

"Willie! " Jason called and glanced at Willie and Willie nodded. They knew they had to run. Willie lunged at Flaco. He doubled down like a blocker while the hissing blade cut empty air over his head then he grabbed Flaco's leg and lifted him off the ground. He threw him over his shoulders and ran.

At the same time Jason kicked out and the gun exploded. The bullet whined over his head and Sapo went down, cursing and holding his numbed hand. Frankie wasn't quick enough for Jason who broke free and ran.

Somewhere down the park somebody called " ¡Chin-gaaaaa-sos! " And the pistol shot ignited the rumble that had been brewing all day.

Sapo cursed and the rage he felt made him forget the pain in his arm. He managed to load the zip pistol, then steadying his arm, he took aim at the fleeing pair.

"No! Sapo! " Frankie shouted and grabbed Sapo's arm. "We'll get them later! Look! " He held Sapo and pointed in the direction of the squad cars. He knew if they were found with the pistol it would mean a bad jail rap.

"He broke my hand! " Sapo shouted savagely as he wrestled free of Frankie. "Nobody ever hits el Sapo! " he cursed, and then because Jason and Willie were already disappearing beyond the trees, he turned his wrath on Frankie. He struck out and the butt of the pistol caught Frankie on the jaw and stretched him out. Sapo stood over him and pointed the pistol at Frankie's forehead. "You let them get away you sonofabitch! " He swore and pulled the trigger. The pin clicked against the bullet, but it didn't fire. Frankie moaned and felt himself wet his pants. "A dud! You got a dud! " Sapo cried and his anger changed to spasms of uncontrolled laughter.

Frankie got up slowly. He felt like striking out, but he was too weak. He let Flaco pull both of them away.

Jason and Willie had skirted the cop cars and disappeared into Barelas. Through the alleys they reached Willie's house. It was an old adobe house with a high fence guarding it. Willie reached through the bramble and vines which grew against the fence and opened a hidden gate. He led Jason into a backyard full of junk. "I told the teachers at school my dad's a collector——" Willie smiled as he pointed to the tall piles of junk that was piled high on either side of the narrow path. Jason followed Willie through the maze. "See here," Willie paused, "here's one of the first Victrola's ever made . . . someday it will be worth something . . . In a shed in the back he's got an original Model-A, in fine condition, and he's got Indian bowls and blankets, old books, violins, everything you can think of——"

"Does he sell any of it? " Jason asked.

Willie looked startled. "Oh no, my dad would never sell any of his stuff, uh-huh."

"Why does he collect it? "

Willie stopped. "I don' know . . . I guess everybody collects something, don't they? When my dad finds something nice, I mean something really nice, not just an old refrigerator or stove, he brings it in the house and he lets all of us look at it and touch it and he tells us a story about it. His eyes light up because then he makes us happy, and even my mother smiles——" He stopped short. "Look, the whole family's like that! I mean . . ."

"I know, Willie, you don't have to explain anything," Jason interrupted and he looked at Willie and let him know it was all right.

"Good," Willie smiled and breathed deep. "Come on, I'll let

65

you meet Henry . . ." He led Jason through the maze to the back of the house where a dark, naked figure sat on an Army cot beneath the giant elm tree. A chain tied at Henry's ankle held him to the elm tree at the end of a ten foot tether. When he saw Willie Henry leaped forward and embraced him. "Will-eeee! " he shrieked joyfully and grunted.

"Hey! Hey! " Willie wrestled him and touseled his long hair. "Lookee here! " He pointed at Jason and Henry reached out. Jason held back. "It's okay! " Willie assured him, "he won't hurt you . . . He knows you're with me; wrestle him down! " So Jason let Henry grab him and wrestle him to the ground. He tried to break his hold, but once Henry held him in his bear-hug Jason couldn't break the grip. "Strong, ain't he? " Willie laughed, and he pulled Henry back.

"Damn right," Jason dusted himself. "We ought to turn him on Sapo, that would cure him! "

"Hey! You're right! " Willie slapped his hands and howled with laughter, and dark, sinewy Henry laughed with him. They sat on the cot and rested and talked and all the while Willie stroked Henry's matted hair. Henry lay contentedly at his feet and listened to them.

"He loves to play," Willie said, "he waits for me to come home so we can wrestle, and he likes for me to tell him stories. I told him about you . . . that you're my friend, and that you came from far away . . . of course, he doesn't understand everything, but I know he likes you, otherwise he'd pick you up and toss you away . . ."

"He's strong enough," Jason agreed. He looked at the chain on Henry's ankle and asked Willie why he was tied.

"When he gets loose he climbs the fence, then the kids of the neighborhood like to chase him and throw rocks at him, and they get their dogs on him . . . See the scar on his leg? A year ago they ran a pack of dogs on him and they nearly tore his leg off, cut his tendons so he's got this limp when he walks . . . so we have to keep him tied up. Another thing he loves to do is go over to la 'cequia, we don't know why but he likes to go there at night and we're afraid he'll drown . . ."

There was a long pause in their conversation. The late summer sun was setting and with it a quiet peace came over the barrio.

What had happened at the park a few hours earlier was far behind them now. The first tinge of autumn suddenly reached out and made them shiver.

"——Is there anything that can be done for him? "

"Nah, not really. We tried it when he was younger, used to take him to doctors and everything, but those welfare quacks didn't give a shit. All they'd do is give him tranquilizers and make him dopey as hell. They said that made him safe, hell man, he's always been safe! Henry doesn't even hurt the flies and ants that crawl over him, and he has never hurt my smaller brothers and sisters. Also, the neighbors forced us to put him away once, cause they said he was dangerous, so they got a petition and made us take him to Las Vegas, but man, he nearly died there. He got sad and wouldn't eat, and when my dad and I went to see him we knew he'd die of sadness if he had to stay. So my dad agreed to keep him chained if we could keep him with us where we could take care of him . . . I think it's the only agreement my dad has ever made with any men, but he did it for Henry . . . It's better this way, he's chained but he's with us and he's happy—— Hey, come on inside and meet my dad."

Willie led him through the back door which was painted a bright blue and into a small, dark kitchen. The disheveled figure of a woman fled into another room when she saw Jason; the big man at the table turned to greet them. He was unshaven and coarse looking, and he frowned when he saw Jason.

"What's this? " he scowled.

"This is my friend, Jason," Willie answered. "I wanted him to meet you——"

The woman that had fled peered around the door. A cluster of ragged kids clung to her skirts and their wide eyes suspiciously inspected Jason.

"My father's name is Rufus," Willie said.

"Humph," Rufus grunted, "why did you bring him? You never brought any of your other friends——"

"Jason's different," Willie shrugged, "he understands . . ."

Rufus eyed Jason, then he got up slowly and walked to him. For a time he looked at Jason and didn't speak. Then the frown left his face and he held out his hand. "People don't often come into the house of Rufus," he said softly, "they are afraid of the dog-killer, the sun worshiper, as they call me. But you are welcome. If you are a friend of my son you are welcome . . ." He looked at Willie and placed his huge hand on his shoulder. "Our house is your house," he said simply.

Later, as he walked home, Jason thought about Willie and his family. They were no more insane than other people, but because they wanted to keep their son Henry with them they had been driven into isolation. And so there were forces that drove men further into themselves, unnatural forces that made a man retreat into himself. He thought about his father and the loneliness he must feel as he found himself separated from his family and the men of the barrio. He thought about Benjie, closing himself off with clouds of marijuana smoke. How does a man break those chains of isolation and loneliness, he wondered, and he looked at the people moving up and down Barelas Road and wondered if the answer lay with them. In the tree-dappled light of the afternoon he felt a flow of energy in the barrio street, like the force of the river in Gualdalupe when it rushed full with summer rain.

CHAPTER SEVEN

Ana decided not to return to school that fall. Juanita tried to persuade her to finish school but Ana laughed and said she didn't need a high school diploma to be a waitress. She got a job at the Coney Island downtown and in the afternoon she and Juanita walked home together.

"But you can go on and do other things if you only stay in school and finish," Juanita argued.

"Like what? " Ana asked cynically.

"Anything you want to do! You can be a teacher, a nurse——"

"Bullshit! " Ana laughed. "Look at yourself. You got your high school diploma and where did it get you, huh? You're a clerk selling cosmetics at Payless, selling junk to women who come to cover the truth! "

Juanita winced. The truth hurt her. She knew Ana looked to her for leadership and she hadn't been able to provide any. Deep inside she felt as trapped as Ana.

"I'm sorry," Ana apologized, "I didn't mean to say you don't have a good job, you do . . . But I need to work too. I like having my own money, and freedom. School is so damn boring I'll go crazy if I have to go back, and besides, mamá needs the help too. I don't know what's happened lately, but it seems we barely get along . . ."

"I know," Juanita nodded. She too had worried about the trouble at the shops and the tension at home that seemed to be splitting the family.

Ana continued pensively. "You know, sometimes I think that everyone in the barrio is selling junk, little bits and pieces of junk, and all the stuff that's really worthwhile is out there somewhere. Somebody else owns the good things, and they sure as hell don't part with them."

Juanita agreed. She understood what Ana was saying, and she liked her directness. For years it seemed that her younger sister had merely followed, now she was discovering herself, and what she encountered she dealt with directly.

"——That's why I like the pachucos," Ana continued, "because when they see junk they call it junk. They don't bullshit around. They understand the world they live in, and they call it like it is. Funny, when we moved here last summer I was afraid of them, now that I understand them and understand the barrio I know why they are like they are——"

Ana identified closely with the pachuco brotherhood, the carnalismo of the barrio. She adopted the pachuca's style, the language, and she had gone as far as tatooing a blue India ink dot on her forehead. With that she had sealed her independence and had begun to move from the circle of the familia to a wider identification within the pachuco movement in the barrio. Juanita also had moved in that direction, but she had come to a standstill, a point from where she looked around her and evaluated the things that had meaning to her life. So, she questioned more than Ana.

"——I guess what I liked most about the pachucos was the excitement," she said. "I thought that because of the way they dressed and talked and because they played around with dope that they were free. I mean, I thought that because they broke all the old rules that they didn't have any rules of their own, but they do. They've just exchanged one set of rules for another——"

"What do you mean? " Ana asked.

"Well, when I first met Chuey I felt as if I was talking to a liberator, someone who was out to break all the rules and create a new way of living. Maybe I expected too much, but it is true that they don't accept the old ways. They've changed the language, the way they dress, everything. They say they aren't afraid and that they will fight against oppression, but then they turn around and create their own rules and regulations that are almost the same as the old ones. For example, I'm not expected to be seen with other men as long as I'm dating Chuey, but he can go out and drink and have a good time whenever he wants to. He can come and go as he pleases, but not me. I swear, I'm not even expected to think? "

They paused in front of the federal building to buy a handful of

70

piñones from the blind woman who sat on the steps. It was after work, and they were on their way home, joining the other workers who moved down Fourth Street towards the barrio. They passed in front of Mori's barbershop and macho-whistles dripping with saliva greeted them.

"Wow! Hey, baby! " "Que chula——" " ¡Mira que cosas hace Dios! "

Juanita and Ana laughed. They called the sidewalk in front of the barbershop the war zone, and when they were past it they jokingly gave thanks to God.

"That's all men ever think about," Ana grinned.

"——Always thinking they have to prove themselves. Pobrecitos, I feel sorry for them." They joked and ran the rest of the way home, feeling in good spirits because it was Saturday night and tonight there was a dance. They arrived in time for supper and because they were all together they enjoyed talking and kidding with each other.

Adelita was especially happy. Lately it seemed as if her familia was seldom together, so even though Clemente had not yet arrived she served supper and took joy in serving them.

"Eat! Eat! " She prodded Benjie, "You're getting so thin you're going to blow away! "

"He's in love," Ana teased her brother, "I've seen him with that girl they call Proxie——"

"You mean Flaco's sister? " Juanita acted surprised, "Oh, you better watch out, Benjie, she's liable to have a jealous brother! And I hear that Flaco's pretty good with a knife——"

Benjie smiled, "Nah, not me, I'm not interested in women. I only take her to the movies once in awhile to give the poor girl a break——"

"Oh-sí, to give her a break! " They razzed him and they all laughed.

Jason didn't say anything. He knew Benjie was dating Flaco's sister. The word on the street was that Benjie was pushing junk for Sapo and his boys. Jason figured that's why they hadn't come after him again.

"You want to know who the real lover is, ask the silent one," Benjie smiled and nodded towards Jason, "I hear he spends a lot of time around the Country Club——"

71

"The Country Club? Ooo-la-la! What's her name? " Juanita asked.

"Cindy," Benjie answered, "es gabachita . . ."

"No kidding! " Ana exclaimed, "What's the matter, Jason, ain't the girls from the barrio good enough for you? " she asked sarcastically.

"Ah, what does Benjie know," Jason shook his head and smiled, "I was at the girl's place once . . ."

"Visiting the Country Club! " Ana continued her prodding, "Boy, you better learn your place. Don't you know what happens to barrio boys who date those rich girls? Why they're liable to cut off your——"

"Enough! " Adelita interrupted. "Leave him alone. At least he comes home at night, and he doesn't run around with marijuanos——" She looked at Benjie and bit her lower lip.

"Mamá! " Benjie flashed a smile, "I told you, I'm busy, I'm working . . ."

"But where? And why so late? I can't sleep until you return, I can't sleep until each of you has returned . . ." She sighed.

Benjie changed the subject. "Well, if it's not la gabachita, it's that girl from Williams, what's her name? Cristina . . . yeah, what a beauty, caray! "

"Another one! " Juanita smiled, "Ah, you can't trust these quiet ones! "

"She's the daughter of the man who got killed this summer, Sánchez . . ."

"She's a nice girl," Adelita said, "I met her mother at church. Everyone should be as lucky to meet a nice girl, and not run with those wild girls . . ."

"Mamá," Benjie smiled, "I don't run with wild girls; I'm too busy for girls." He stood to leave.

"Where are you going? " Adelita asked.

"I gotta meet some friends," Benjie answered. He went to her and kissed her forehead. "Don't worry about me, I'm all right . . ."

"It's just that we haven't been together for so long," Adelita said, "and your father will be home soon. Why don't you stay a while so we can all be together again! "

Benjie stiffened. "I can't, mamá, I promised to meet these friends . . . I gotta see them about a job . . ." He smiled and called adiós and went out laughing.

"¡Que Dios te bendiga! " Adelita called after him. She sipped coffee and said, "Oh, I worry about him . . . those friends he has . . ."

"They're okay," Ana said, "there's nothing to worry about. He likes to have fun, that's all . . ." She held her mother's hand to reassure her, but they couldn't look in her eyes because they knew the truth.

They had just finished eating when Clemente arrived. He was drunk and in a bad mood. He had been drinking for weeks, but the liquor could no longer cover the sense of alienation and frustration he felt and tonight it boiled over in anger he couldn't contain. "Where's my supper? " he shouted and banged on the table.

Adelita quickly reheated the meal and served him. She understood why he had been drinking and she knew the best way to handle it was to say nothing, but tonight he was unusually drunk. She motioned for Jason to leave the kitchen; she didn't like for her children to see their father drunk. But Jason also sensed his father's hostility, so he lingered at the door. There was a bad feeling in the air, something he had never felt before but which he knew had been building up during the past few weeks.

"Your supper is ready," Adelita said softly. Clemente looked at it and scowled, then pushed it away.

"And where is my family? " he cried out. "Is the man of the house to eat alone! Like a dog! I want my family around me when I eat! " His soul was heavy with sentimiento and the drink had only served to bring his hurt to the surface. Now he would cover his feelings further by asserting himself. And as his wrath concealed the real reason for his drinking, it also sought out another cause which he could blame for the sense of alienation he felt from his family.

"Clemente," Adelita tried to calm him, "Jasón and I are here, and your daughters are in their room, getting ready for the dance. We are all here——"

"A dance! " He exclaimed, "There is a dance tonight and they have not asked my permission! I have not given them permission to go the dance! "

"You were not here——" Adelita tried to explain.

"Well, I am here now! Let my daughters come before me, and

73

let them ask permission of the father, as it should be! " He commanded his wife.

"Clemente," she answered quietly, "I have already given them permission to go——"

"You! " He cried angrily, "You cannot give them permission! Since when does the woman play the man's part! " He jumped up and shook his fist in her face. "You are turning my family away from me! That's what you're doing! I know why they no longer come to me, because behind my back you plan against me! You turn them against me! Well, we will take care of that right now——" He cursed and staggered into the girls' bedroom.

The liquor had finally pushed him over the hurdle of inaction. It was a false courage, but he didn't care. He would use it to reassert himself. Somehow he had lost command over his life and destiny. He had spent hours during the past few weeks in the bar, seeking in alcohol a reason for his loneliness and impotence. A world he once ruled had suddenly slipped away from him, and a wedge had been driven between himself and his family. First he blamed the city and the alienation he felt in it, and he cursed the politics of the shops which were splitting the men into different camps, and tonight he lashed out against his wife. In his alcoholic stupor he turned against the person closest to him. He saw her plotting with the other forces that were set on destroying his position as head of the family. She had grown stronger since their arrival in the city, while he had grown weaker. She was now in control of the finances of the family, and he had to beg or steal from her just to buy a drink.

In his anguish and desperation he saw her turning his family away from him. They no longer came to him for advice or leadership; he felt they no longer needed him. She had defended Benjie and swore by all the saints that he wasn't smoking marijuana, while everybody knew the truth. She defended her daughters and said they had the right to come and go as they pleased, as long as *she* knew where they were going, and she insisted that the pachucos they dated were not marijuanos. She would ruin his family if he didn't put a stop to her meddling and reaffirm his rightful place, and so he hounded his daughters out of their bedroom and into the kitchen.

He pushed them into a corner and cried out furiously, "How

74

dare you plan to go out without asking your father's permission! Is this what your upbringing has taught you? To disobery your father! " He glared at them, expecting their resistance and defiance, and instead Juanita tore away from his grip and very calmly asked, "May we go to the dance, papá? "

For a moment he felt thwarted. He felt one more slap in the face from a world that had already driven him to exasperation. He felt he had to make his stand and fight here, or else the energy to do it would never come again.

"No! " He shook his head, "you cannot go——" Then searching for an alternative command that would lend him support he ordered them to sit and eat with him.

"But, Clemente," Adelita protested, "the girls have already eaten, everyone has eaten——"

" ¡Ay! ¡Vívora! " He lashed out, "You encourage your children not to obey their father! Since we came to this cursed city you have plotted to separate me from my family, and now you do it openly! "

"That is not true, Clemente," Adelita cried, "how can you say such horrible things! You have been drinking, you do not know what you say—— Please, Clemente, leave the children alone," she pleaded with him, "go to bed, tomorrow you will see——"

"Bah! " He pushed her aside. "I see everything perfectly clear now. I see my daughters disobey me, and I see my own wife encourage that disobedience! You say I have been drinking," he laughed bitterly, "and that is true. But I see clearly enough, I see what you have done. You allow my own daughters to run loose like whores——"

"Clemente! For the love of God! " Adelita cried out. "Do not use language like that in front of the children! " She shook her head in disbelief. She knew what was tearing at him and why he was drinking, but she had never expected that he would blame her for it. She did not understand the fury of his onslaught. He was a different man from the husband she once knew.

"I will use any language I want! I am the man of this house! " He shouted. "I pay the rent! I buy the groceries! Therefore I will make the rules! "

He saw fear in their eyes, and that spurred him on. Perhaps it was working, perhaps he was regaining the control he thought he had lost. Maybe he had been too weak; now he had to rule with an iron hand. He would make the rules, and they would obey! For a moment he felt a surge of power fill his body and clean away the cobwebs of the alcohol. He would control again; he would rule again!

"We work too, papá! " Juanita struck back, "we have our own money, and we help pay the rent! "

"Yes! " Ana was right beside her, "and you have no right to treat us like whores! You are drunk and making a fool of yourself! Grosero——"

" ¡Sinvergüenza! " Juanita added. "How can we respect and obey you when you treat us like dirt! "

The agony of the insult twisted in his stomach and made him quiver. For a moment he had felt in control again, now he was worse than a fool, he was nothing. Blinded by that painful realization and by the frustration and impotency he felt he struck back. He grabbed the meat knife from the table and held it over their heads. They shrieked and fell back trembling, huddling together for protection against the madman. Jason jumped in the way to ward off the blow, but it did not come. Clemente realized what he had almost done. He stumbled back and fell into a chair. The knife dropped from his trembling hand.

" ¡Dios mío! ¡Dios mío! " He shook his head and groaned. He covered his face with his hands and sobbed. Adelita quickly pulled her daughters away. The bedroom door closed behind them. For a long time Clemente sat at the table, mumbling, and then he stumbled to his bed. The house grew dark; the women whispered in the bedroom. Jason sat in the porch and listened while he stared blankly down Barelas Road.

"He's crazy," he heard Ana say.

"No, it was the wine. He's been drinking a lot——"

"He's going to kill himself if he keeps on drinking."

"We should have called the police," Ana declared. "The next time he does something like that I am going to call them! "

"It's not his fault," Adelita intoned. "He needs to feel that he is needed, that he is still the head of the family, and he doesn't know how. He can't bear to know that you support me, us——"

"But we only help you, mamá," Juanita said, "he has his job——"

Adelita shook her head. "He's been out of work since school started," she admitted. "He didn't want you to know——"

"Out of work! " Juanita exclaimed in surprise, "But how, why? "

"It's a long story——" Adelita sat at the bedside and told what she knew. "You know that the workers at the shops have been trying to form a new union. The one they have is corrupt; it is run by a man called Kirk; apparently he is chosen by the bosses and he can stay in office as long as he keeps the workers in line. They are afraid to demand their rights because they lose their jobs, and jobs are scarce, it is not like during the war when everyone could work and wages were good. So, the workers have no rights, no way of deciding their security and wages. If they speak out, they are fired, that is the kind of power the bosses give Kirk.

"Well, some of the men won't stand for that. They want to have their own union, they want to elect their own union president, a man who will speak for the workers and their rights—— so they called a meeting. Clemenete is not a troublemaker, he is not a politician, but he is a man that knows that to live he must remain free in his own heart. He began to see how mistreated the workers were, and he did not like that. So he went to the meeting. There was only a small group of them at first, but they took over the union hall, and as their numbers increased Kirk grew afraid and told them they couldn't use the building. He said they were all radicals, misled by the man they call Lalo, and he threatened to fire them all.

"He began pushing them out of the building, threatening them, and the men obeyed, because they have been under his whip for so long. Well, he made the mistake of pushing your father. No man has ever pushed your father. He struck back, and as Roberto explained it, now they call that crooked man el Kirk sin dientes—— Ay! But his bite is worse than ever! He fired your father from his work, and he also let go many of the other men who had called the meeting. And the power of those shop bosses goes far, so the men can't find work even in the city; everywhere jobs are closed to them. Most are moving back to their ranchitos or the small towns they came from. But your father cannot go back, don't you see, we keep him here. And he has nowhere to turn, and so——"

77

"He has been drinking," Juanita finished.

"You should have told us," Ana added.

"He would not let me," Adelita shook her head. "He is too proud. Oh, don't ask me what a poor man has to be proud of, I don't know. It is a part of his will, a part of who he is. It flows from his name, and from the earth itself. Yes, I remember when we were young and just married, I remember watching the Chávez brothers walk on that llano-land of theirs. My God, you would have sworn that they were gods themselves the way they held themselves and walked upon that earth. It is something that can never be destroyed, and at the same time it is that pride that destroys him now. He is too proud to admit to anyone that he needs help, and he would rather destroy himself by drinking than let anyone give him charity——

"You see," she spoke earnestly to her daughters, "once there would have been the land to make him whole again. A man who met deafeat could go out on the land, and the earth would make him well again. It might take weeks, or months, or years, but always the man who looked found himself in his earth, and he was well. And there were also the people, los compadres, los vecinos, the people of the small pueblos, they understood and lent their support, so a man was never lost, never separated from his soul." Her eyes filled with tears. She touched her apron to her nose and stood up. "Now, well, things have changed, and your father, he is a man lost in a foreign land——"

"And you, mamá?" Juanita asked and put her hand on her mother's shoulder.

Adelita smiled. "I am never lost if my familia is around me," she answered. "There have been good times, and there have been hard times," she added. "There have been times of joy and thanksgiving, and times of sadness and misery . . . and there were the good times of our youth . . . ah, but that was so long ago, and in a different time and place . . ." She stood to leave. She thought for a moment about the love she and Clemente had shared on the llano when they were young. Many things had changed, but she loved him still, and she would not leave his side when he needed her. "—— Finish dressing and go to the dance, enjoy yourselves," she said to her daughters, "and try to forget you saw your father at his worst. If God permits, someday you will see his great-

78

ness . . ."

She walked swiftly to the door and closed it behind her. She went to her husband's side and listened for a moment. He was sprawled on the bed and snoring. She looked at him and smiled. Once he had been young and filled her nights with eternity, and the beautiful corridos of love he sang had not been sour with wine. Ah, how soon we forget the poems of our youth, she thought, and removed his shoes and dirty socks. She pulled his legs up on the bed and covered him with a blanket so the cool autumn air wouldn't chill him. He turned and mumbled something, and she placed her cool hand on his forehead and whispered, "Aquí estoy."

I am here. Sleep.

CHAPTER EIGHT

In the fall a wildcat strike racked the shops. Kirk, the union boss, had fixed the vote on the new contract and reported ratification by the union. Lalo and his group demanded a recount but the ballots had already been burned. The men took to the streets; instant pickets went up around the shops. But the group was small and without the support of the entrenched union leadership there was little they could do. By the end of the day the dissenters were declared workers without seniority, absentee and on-the-job irregularities were trumped up against them and they were fired. The few jobs created were quickly filled and the railroad was triumphant in its classic move to break the strike by splitting the workers. The act was smoothly accomplished with the help of the corrupt union leader.

The men that did not heed the call to strike made excuses and went on working. What could a man do? A lousy job was better than no job in the tightening recession. And if the union leadership couldn't be challenged by a man as forceful as Lalo why should they stick their necks out.

"Because the only way we're going to get a decent contract is to unite! " Lalo shouted at the scabs that crossed the line. "We've got to throw out Kirk and his cronies! They're not serving us, they're serving themselves! "

The men who crossed the line buried their shoulders deeper into their jackets. They knew what Lalo said was true, but it seemed hopeless to fight for better salaries and working conditions when times were so bad. And the fast retribution of the railroad made them leery. The company union was in cahoots with the railroad officials and the worker was at the bottom of the pile when it came to having any rights. But there seemed little the aborted strike had done to crack that alliance, so the workers that had not gone out initially were glad they still had a job.

It was a dismal gray morning when they crossed the line the following day. Lalo and his group were at the gate, cajoling them to stay out. When they went through he cursed them.

"Hey! Remember Sánchez! " he called out in the thin misty rain, "What the hell did they do for him, huh! Nothing! And what about Juan Loco! He lost ten fingers and now he's dancing for free drinks at the bar! Remember him! "

The men returning to work passed by quickly, turning aside to shut off his shouts.

" ¡Cabrones lambes! " Héctor cursed. He was Lalo's right hand. "You're working under a contract that doesn't carry your vote! " he shouted. No one listened. The small band of strikers turned to Lalo; they had gone out with him and they had lost their jobs, now they turned to him for leadership.

"We meet tonight," he encouraged them. "Bring everyone, even those that are still working. We'll make them see the wrong! I'll have a lawyer there; we'll take all of those pinches to jail . . . I swear someday we're going to be strong enough not to have to ask for our rights, but to demand our rights! "

Clemente was at the back of the small group that stood in the rain that morning. No one noticed him, and they did not pay any attention to him when they met that night. A large group met in the local bar and listened to the lawyer explain the various avenues they could take. In the end they were dissatisfied. The law was an entanglement of suits and procedures and the process described by the lawyer was long and drawn out. What the men wanted was work and the formation of a new union that would protect their rights.

"What are we goin' do now! " A man shouted when the lawyer was through talking.

"Unite! " Lalo shouted. "The only way we change anything is to stand together! "

"Unite! " the men echoed his call.

"We need more advice than that smart-ass lawyer had to give us with his fancy words! " a man at the back of the room shouted. "We need advice from someone who understands our problems! Did you go to the priest for help! "

Some of the men hooted. Lalo laughed contemptuously.

"Yes, I went to the padrecito this morning to see if we could use the gym for our meeting tonight, but he said it was being used for bingo! " The men laughed in derision.

"They're playing bingo with beans," a man said, "and the padre doesn't realize our people are stealing the beans to eat! " The men howled with laughter, but when the laughter subsided they looked at each other nervously.

"—— I asked him for the church and he almost fainted," Lalo continued. "He said it was unheard of to organize a strike in a church. He called me a communist and ran me out," Lalo spit. "So we meet here," he finished cynically and waved his arm to indicate the smoke-filled car.

"We can't expect help from anyone! " Héctor shouted. "We've got to picket the shops and bring them to the negotiating table! That's the only way they'll listen to us! "

"But we're not a union," a fellow worker reminded him. "No one would honor our pickets, and we'd probably be thrown in jail for breaking the law. What we should do is work with the union we already have, file our grievances with it——"

"And where in the hell did that ever get us! " Lalo shouted anrgily. "We've filed grievance after grievance, and Kirk wipes his ass with them. He can't buck the system, they appointed him! "

"It's true! " The men shouted. "Organize! " A great cry went up as the men called for action.

"Wait a minute! Wait! " Old Manuel stood up and called for order. "Okay, so you want to organize, that's good, but sonamagon first you have to elect a leader. You will need a spokesman, someone who can deal with Kirk and the shop bosses——"

The men nodded in agreement. What Manuel had said was true. They needed a leader, and at the same time they knew they were not ready to go with Lalo. They did not understand Lalo's thinking and so they did not completely trust him. And if they could not place their complete trust in him the strike was doomed to failure. They did not understand Lalo because he spoke of violence, he preached a revolution that would wrench power away from the bosses. Lalo's doctrine was a process of force; he carried a pistol and he encouraged all the men to arm themselves so that when the time came they could wrest away the power that held them captive in their jobs, and if need be they would destroy themselves and the entire system in the process. Most of the workers shied away from him for that reason.

Manuel continued. "You know that the familia without a strong father soon falls apart, and that a pueblo without a good leader is not united in its effort to serve the people, and a country without a good, strong man to guide it is soon overrun by its enemies. Our own revolutions have taught us the value of a wise leader, now we must find that man among ourselves——"

He paused and looked out over the group. The men shifted uneasily. No one rose and no names were offered. They were not yet ready to entrust their power to a spokesman. Many small conversations started as the small groups at each table discussed the same question: Who was the leader to be? On one side men gathered around Lalo and encouraged him to take the leadership position, but on the other side the majority of the men still held back. The initial meeting ended without resolution, but not in discord, and so one of the men called to Crispín to sing them a song that would help bring them together again.

"Play, Crispín, play of things as they are, or things as they have been——"

Crispín strummed the blue guitar. He sang the corridos of prior revolutions, he sang of ancient heroes, men of the people. The mystery of his melody and the magic of his words carried them out of their present time and misery to a time of legends and myths, and in that time he made them encounter the truth of their being.

"...We are the fruit of the people who wandered from the mythical land of Aztlán, the first people of this land who wandered south in search of a sign."

The men relaxed and listened. They knew the story, but they listened reverently to the blind poet. The notes of the blue guitar danced on the dense smoke and drew the men together.

"Tell us the meaning of the sign," Clemente begged. The legend and the names were new to him.

"It is a simple story," Crispín continued, "a burning god fell from the sky and told the people to travel southward. The sign for which they were to watch was a giant bird in whose claws would be ensnared the poisonous snakes which threatened the people. In that place, under the protection of that plumed bird, the

83

wanderers from Aztlán were to build their new civilization. There they would meet the second part of their destiny—— But the important thing," Crispín leaned forward so all could listen, "is to know how to interpret the signs. The legend renews itself with each generation, and we must know how to unravel the meaning of the sign——"

"Ah, there is a meaning! " Clemente whispered. He felt himself shiver, and the sweat on his forehead turned cold. When he was young he had worked on the llano and listened to the stories of the old man who could fly, and now Crispín's story rang with the same sense of mystery he had heard long ago. "What is the meaning of this sign? " he asked. The room grew silent. The bartender left off washing dishes, and two whores at the bar also turned and listened.

"There is a meaning in all the stories of *the people,*" Crispín smiled, "that is why we cannot let those legends die . . . Think on it, my friends, think of the exodus of *the people* from Aztlán . . . It is a story which far surpasses the wanderings of the Jews of the Bible, it is an odyssey where gods visited with men as they once did in the stories of ancient Greece . . . there is passion, and there is tragedy, and there are the foundings of civilizations that equal those of the old world . . . and all of it here, on this earth, on this land of Aztlán . . ."

"But the strike? The strike and the railroad? What do these stories have to do with that? " Clemente pressed forward.

Crispín sang, and in his song the winding trains were like the thrashing, poisonous serpents, and while one was born of the earth the other was born from the imagination of the foreigners to the east . . . Shadows with forms, he called them, monsters that have spread over the earth to enslave the people. "But oooh, there was a protector once before; a giant bird sent by the guardian sun, a bird to mate the snake and steal its fear! So now we need a man who will rise like the eagle and melt the power of the steel snakes! The soul of the people is trapped in steel and the cry is for the man who will let them go! "

"Freedom! " Lalo's group shouted as they were swept up by the old man's words.

"Strike now and destroy the chains that bind us! "

"But how? " old Manuel asked in frustration. "The old monsters were shadows and dreams; these modern snakes of steel are a thousandfold more evil and powerful! "

"Where will a man find that power to melt the steel? "

"In his heart . . ." Crispín crooned, "in the heart of Aztlán . . ."

"But where is this place called Aztlán? " Clemente persisted, but the story was done, the men were spent. They shook their heads in disbelief and turned to finish their drinks.It was a beautiful story, they all agreed, and the legend of the past had been fulfilled, but that was long ago when things like that happened. Times had changed, things were different now, and so they listened to the old man because the cuentos were a part of their heritage and because the stories for a moment ripped the veil of reality; but that was all; when the story was done the grime and poverty of the barrio enveloped them again and they understood the intriguing story did not get them back their jobs. The stories of the past didn't put beans and meat on the table for the family. Sure the stories helped to pass the time and ease the despair of going jobless that winter, but that was all.

Only Clemente's torment increased as the story unfolded, and when Crispín was done he pushed through the milling crowd, but when he reached the place where Crispín had sat the old man was gone. Clemente searched the crowd which was drifting out, but Crispín was not to be seen. So he returned to a table in a dark corner to drink alone. He sought out the oblivion which he had learned to find in liquor, but tonight he couldn't find rest. The images of Crispín's story kept appearing before him and try as he might to push them away they returned to haunt him. There was something very true and very essential in the story and it kept calling to him to find its meaning. He was bound up with the people of the story, and with the legend of the eagle and the serpent, and all that related somehow to him and to the strikers who sought justice, but he didn't know how. And the place called Aztlán was like a mysterious word, latent with power, stretching from the dark past to the present to ring in his soul and make him tremble.

"Where was this place called Aztlán? And did the word mean heart of the earth? " he asked himself as he paid for his drinks and stumbled into the cold, midnight darkness.

Another thing disturbed him as he walked down the empty

85

streets. When the men called for a leader some of them had looked in his direction. Why should they look at me, Clemente cursed, I don't give a damn for their politics! All I ever did was hit Kirk in the mouth . . . "Leave me alone! " he shouted to the shadows, and still they haunted him and drove him restlessly towards a dark corner of Barelas.

Suddenly he stopped and remembered that there were certain spots of earth on the wide llano where he had once stood and felt the elation of flying! Yes, the power of the earth surged through him until he felt himself soaring over the landscape. Perhaps that is what Crispín meant when he said a man could fly like the guardian bird of the legend.

He stopped at a street corner and leaned against a light pole. Old memories of the llano flooded his troubled mind. He had gone once to the old sheepherder they called el hombre volador, and he had asked the man if he could explain this strange feeling. The old man had laughed and said that the dark secrets of the earth were only for those who were willing to search to the very core and essence of their being.

"I am ready now! " Clemente shouted, and the murky winds of the night slapped his words away and left silence ringing in his ears. A wave of nausea passed over him and left him trembling, and he cursed his weakness. Then he remembered that the old man had said to make the trip a man should be without fear and that he needed a spiritual guide, because in the end the man who sought had everything to gain, and everything to lose. Clemente had laughed then; he had too much to lose. Now he had nothing.

"There must be someone! " he cried. Perhaps the old woman Crispín had talked about the night they met. Yes, she had the power of that strange rock, and she could tell the future. He would ask her if he was the man to lead the workers, and either way the answer came he would at least be rid of the anxiety that nagged at him. He turned and stumbled towards the river. He thought he found the place, but the darkness was so thick and dense his resolution failed him and he grew fearful. He turned to go back but he was lost. He wandered in circles and cursed as he fought back the brush that whipped at him, and the more he struggled to free himself the denser the thicket grew and the more it enveloped him. He cursed himself for coming. He had never known fear and yet he was ready to call for help when he heard the sound of running water. He remembered la 'cequia ran through the bosque, and so he lunged towards the sound of water. The canal ran towards the bridge; he could follow it and be free of the suffocating darkness. He pushed frantically through the brush and was nearly at the water's edge when he tripped and fell short. When he looked up he saw something that made him freeze and hold his breath. There, dancing across a small clearing by the water, reeled the figure of a dark, naked man. At first Clemente thought it was a shadow of the tree-dappled light of the moon, but when the shadow spoke terror gripped Clemente's throat. He watched helplessly as the figure reached the middle of the clearing. There the naked man raised his arms and cried to the moon.

"Looooo-na . . ." The animal sound broke the dreadful silence. "Luna——" the naked man cried playfully to the golden disc, and the autumn moon responded. She freed herself from the dark clouds and momentarily bathed the dark man with her golden rays. He danced in circles of delight and called her name in simple adoration.

A scream of terror exploded from Clemente's throat. He jumped up and fought his way through the thick brush, leaving behind him the unperturbed figure praying to the moon. He raced for the dim light of a hut beneath the giant alamos, but as he neared the light a pack of snarling dogs surrounded him. They had whined and cowered when the naked figure of a man passed their way, but now they smelled a frightened man and they tore viciously at his legs. Clemente turned to fight off the savage pack when he heard his name whispered. A bony hand touched his shoulder and he turned and saw the cloaked figure of the old women who kept the magic rock. She hissed and the dogs backed away, then whimpering they disappeared into the shadows. She turned and beckoned, and he followed her into her mud hut.

A sputtering candle made the shadows dance on the walls. An acrid, sulfurous smell filled the room. The shelves of the walls were filled with rotting carcasses of animals; roots and herbs hung in disarray around the room. A small fire glowed in the wood-burning stove where a foul-smelling concoction simmered. The hunchbacked old woman stood in front of the candle and removed her heavy cloak. Clemente gasped as he looked into her face. It was old and shriveled, and seeing her thus sent a shiver through him.

"You seek me? " She asked, and her burning eyes drew him close.

He hesitated, then found the courage to ask, "Are you the woman who keeps the magic rock? "

" ¡La piedra mala! " Her voice cracked with laughter. "So you have finally come to speak to the dark powers . . ." She held him with her piercing stare. "You are no ordinary man, Clemente Chávez, you will have to pay dearly for the answers in the rock! "

"I, I have no money——" Clemente muttered.

"Bah! " she scoffed. "It is not silver we want from you! If you would speak to this ancient and divining stone you must first make a pact with it . . . You must sell your soul! " She turned and swept a black cloth from the table and revealed la piedra mala. It was a black, shiny object which seemed to squirm and pulsate with life as the dark hair which grew on its surface oscillated gently. Clemente felt the nausea of fear shake his body, but still he moved to touch it.

"No! " The old witch held up her bony hand. "You cannot touch it until you make your pact with it! "

Clemente pulled back. "I want to know if I will be the man to lead the workers . . . and where is this place called Aztlán."

"It can tell you everything! " The old woman nodded assuringly. She held out a black hook and said, "Sell your soul to the powers of darkness, and it will answer all your questions! " Her voice rang like dark thunder in his ears.

He had come too far and suffered too much to be kept back, but he would not sell his soul to the devil. It was enlightenment he sought and not damnation. "No! " he cried forcefully and with a surge of strength he pushed the old hag aside and laid his hands on the rock. He had expected to feel a soft, rubbery substance, instead what he touched was hard and jagged. For a moment he felt ecstatic. A warm sensation flowed from the rock through his body and he heard a beautiful, unearthly melody. Then a flash of green fire jumped from the living stone and exploded in his body. He fell back screaming in pain. The force of the electric fire hurled him across the room.

"He-he-he! " The old woman laughed, "Now you have felt the power in the rock! Sell your soul and it will treat you kindly! "

She came upon him, thrusting her black rock at him.

"No! No! " Clemente cried in fright. He stumbled backwards, found the door and ran out. He ran until he found a light and there he sank unconscious to the ground. His body was exhausted by the shock and it could no longer move, but his mind mounted his soul on the wild horses of a pesadilla and they carried him through a night of hell.

When he awoke in the morning he found himself in an alley. His body was numb with pain. He felt the welts where the tree branches had stung and the slashes on his legs where the dogs of night had torn at him. His hands were covered with blisters and he could smell the faint trace of sulfur on them. He got up slowly, afraid that the reality of the shining sun might disappear if he awoke suddenly. He turned and looked towards the river, looking for a clue of the entrance he had found into the dark bosque, but there was none. The pleasant green of the river alamos glittered in the bright sun and birds sang in the shadows. Clemente shivered. He was sure he had touched the power in the old hag's magic rock and he looked at his blistered hands again to assure himself it had not been a dream. So, Crispín was right about these singing rocks, he thought, they existed on earth . . . but how did a man reach into their power to see the heart of the past? And were these rocks the heart of the strange fiery god of the legend or rubble of the earth?

Clemente bent and picked up a stone at his feet. It was a plain, smooth stone, washed down from the mountains hundreds of years ago. There was nothing special to it and yet as he held it in his hands he felt a strange vibration humming in the rock. He looked at the crest of the mountain. Somehow the rock and the mountain were connected. He looked at the grean leaves of the river trees and for a moment he thought he saw the golden strings of light that connected the leaves, the rock, the mountain. The same feeling and driving compulsion that had led him to the old woman the night before swept over him and he trembled. Then as the sensation subsided he cursed and cast the rock aside.

"Why should I think I could ever be the leader of the people! " he spit and cleared his mouth of its bitter coppery taste. "Let others seek to understand what a leader must know . . ." He walked slowly towards Barelas, swearing he would search no further.

CHAPTER NINE

School was a drag. While the teachers droned on about grammar rules and math equations the minds of the students were far astray. Today especially the herds of students could not concentrate; they sat restlessly in their seats and looked at the clock. School was to be dismissed at noon for the students to attend the State Fair, so everybody sat around marking time. Some of the more courageous teachers attempted to give their classes a lecture on the value of the educational experience of the exhibits at the fair, but no one listened. Everyone knew the fair dismissal just meant a half day off from school.

Fair Day was also the day the pachucos and the stompers squared off for a big gang fight before they settled down for the long winter. The pachucos were mostly from the surrounding barrios; the stompers were the kids who dressed like cowboys and who came in on buses from the big ranches along the river valley. They hated each other and most of the fights at school revolved around these two factions. Everyone knew that trouble had been brewing since school started and that the rumble would come today; the tension made the small, colorless classrooms unbearable.

For the vatos the prospects of a half day off for the fair was even more exciting because Pato had just bought a customized '48 Ford. That morning he picked up the gang and showed off by burning rubber up and down the barrio streets. He'd pick up one of the vatos and roar away, leaving behind a billowing cloud of smoke and dust.

"Hey man! Great machine! " The vatos admired the wine-colored, low-riding bomb. "How much did it cost you, ése? "

"It's cool, man! Look at those seat covers! Leopard fuzz! "

When they stopped for Willie he jumped in through the

window, shouting, "Shotgun! Shotgun! "

"Cut it out, Willie! " Pato shouted protectively and reached across to check for scratches on the door. "You do that once more and no rides! " Pato frowned and checked his ducktail in the rear view mirror.

"What's a thing for if not to use," Willie shrugged.

"When'd ju get it? "

"Saturday—and man, do the chicks go wild! I was at the dance at the Center Saturday night, and I could of had my pick——"

"Yeah, and he wound up with Marlene! " Willie laughed.

"What's wrong with Marlene? " Pato defended himself.

"Nothing, except everyone else at la Washa has had her! "

Los vatos laughed and the conquest of the lover of la Washa shrank and soured. "Ah," Pato tossed it off as he double-clutched, "I just gave the chick a break . . . there's better broads than that just waiting to ride up to the West Mesa with me, and man it won't be to see the city lights! " The vatos grinned. Pato would be able to fix himself up easily now that he had wheels.

"How do you know about Marlene? " Dickie asked. "She's in special ed. with me," Willie smiled, "and I know why all the teachers invite Marlene to take inventory of their closets——" he laughed.

"She's built like a brick shithouse, but nothing upstairs," Pete commented.

"Like Willie," Pato added. "All those special ed. kids are like that," he teased Willie and tried to get back at him, "ain't that right, Willie? "

"Ah, we got a lot of fringe benefits," Willie grinned and wiped at his nose. "When I get bored of reading comics I split for PE, that's my favorite class . . . I get to move around a lot, so why complain. I find the interesting classes and sit there till they get boring, then I split. Last year I found a math class that taught me more about math in a few weeks than the rest of you learn in a year. There was a new teacher and he had a fantastic project going! He set up this place so it was like a bank, and each one of us had an account, and we could write checks and borrow money, and we were learning how credit works . . . Man, that's where it's at, credit. And lending money, and interest . . . if you learn that you know how the whole chingadera works! I was learning

91

enough to break el Super if I wanted, and then what happens? The principal came along and told the teacher he didn't have any discipline over us cause we were too excited and noisy, but damn we were learning something! So after that we're back to the same old problems and reading silently in the *Readers Digest* on Fridays ... the principal comes along, smiles, pats the teacher on the back and tells him he's doing a great job. Great! It was boring as hell, so I cut out in search of a new class . . ."

"How'd you get into special ed. in the first place? " Jason asked Willie.

"I told them I was from Barelas! " Willie grinned.

"That's all? "

"Ah, they gave me a big-ass test and I flunked it——"

"He's there because he's off," Dickie shot in.

"Hey, he's not any dumber than the rest of us," Jason defended him. He turned to Willie. "But you could get out now——"

"Now you're acting crazy," Willie smiled. "Look, while the rest of you are locked in classrooms for six periods a day I can come and go as I want ... I can go to different classes, work in the office, go to PE, go down to the basement and play checkers with the janitors, I can do anything ... Cause they think I'm not all there they let me move around, so I've learned the system inside out. I know where the teachers like to go to drink and which of them are messing around, and I know where the principal keeps his little bottle ... I know how to get things done, who to go to, and how to keep out of the way when things are hot ... I've learned how it works; in fact I feel sorry for you poor bastards; you're the ones that are locked up! "

"You're crazy, Willie! " Pete countered. The whole friggin' family's crazy," Pato added, " ¡bien locos! "

"They eat dog meat, that's why," Dickie laughed.

"You lie! " Willie shouted.

" ¡Me la rayo por mi jefita! " Dickie swore. "I saw Rufus kill my dog! One night last summer I heard my dog barking and I got up to see what's the matter, and there's Rufus, Willie's dad, calling my dog, here doggie, doggie, doggie. Then toma! Un chingaso with a club and my dog's in the bag, on his way to be made dog-burgers! " They laughed at Willie.

He responded with one of his shorter curses. "You lie, you

92

tecato, pendejo, grifo, pinche lambe, joto, hijo de Rin Tin Tin liar! "

"Cool it, Willie," Jason calmed him, "we know it's not true. Can't you see they're trying to get you mad——"

"Hell, I know," Willie nodded, "and I don't mind if they pick on me, but why bring my old man into it! He's an honest man, he works hard for a living, and he can't help what happened to our family. It's not his fault, it's just the way things happened. People call us crazy, hell! That just means we don't act like them! We're still human, and he loves us and provides for us. The hardest things is——" He stopped and looked out the window, but they waited for him to finish.

"The hardest thing is not being able to show him that we love him——" he whispered to himself.

They were silent. They didn't look at each other. They cleared their throats and changed the subject.

"Hey, how about chicks! " Pato said and turned to drive around the school so everyone could see his car. "Let's get fixed up and really have a ball this afternoon. We can get some beer and maybe a little mota, and man we can fly high on the roller coaster! "

They laughed and relaxed and waved coolly at friends who loitered on the school grounds.

"Who you taking, Jason? "

"Who else," Chelo winked, "Cristina . . ."

"Cristina? Her old man's the one that got killed this summer," Pato mused; "how in the hell is it Jason winds up with the nice-looking chicks, huh? "

"Some got it, some ain't——"

"He just doesn't waste his time chasing pigs like Marlene," Pete slapped Pato's back and they laughed.

"He hasn't talked to another girl since the party," Chelo kidded his friend, "he eats with her, walks her home . . . toda la fregadera! "

"Hey, you better watch it, Jason, you'll be tied up before you know it! "

"Hey, what about Cindy? " Pato asked. "It was pretty hot there for a while, wasn't it? "

"Nah, there wasn't anything there," Jason shook his head.

93

"Nothing there! " Pato groaned. "Why man, she's the best piece at la Washa! And her old man's got money up the ganootz! Man, whoever she marries is going to be set up for life! Nice chante, Cadillac car, money . . . hey, he'd probably send you up to the university to become a hot-ass lawyer like him! Teach you how to swindle money! "

"You kidding! " Dickie laughed. "Nobody from Barelas ever went up the hill to the university . . ."

"Jason could do it," Willie nodded.

"Hell, any one of us could do it! If we only knew how. You gotta have some backing from the teachers, or somebody——"

"If only somebody would tell us——"

"Ah, screw it! " Pato cut in. "Too many ifs! Who in the hell's going to wait around long enough to get all those ifs straightened out, huh? I'm not." He swung the car into a parking place and they jumped out. "——There's too many other things to do to live on ifs . . ." He smoother his ducktail and popped some Dentyne in his mouth.

"Like women? "

"Yeah! "

"Booze and good times? "

"Yeah! "

"Be-bop music and girls twisting to it? "

"Yeah," Pato smiled and they walked away, "anything else, you can have, but don't sit around asking *what if?* Do it! "

"See you at noon! " they called and went their separate ways.

The morning dragged for Jason. He thought a lot about what Pato had said because it made him think about his own life and what he wanted out of it. Guadalupe was in the past now, and everything associated with it was gone. He remembered the friends he had grown up with and wondered if he would ever see them again. A flood of images burst the channels of silent memory and he saw himself running with Anthony along the river, milling in the herds of kids as they surrounded the school, and running with Ida and June in the windy spring day as they raced to the church to have the priest hear their confessions. Where are they now, he

94

wondered, and have they changed as much as I?

Barelas was a new time and place. The action of the barrio had quickened his pulse and for a while he had worried that he was moving too fast, like Benjie, and then Cristina had entered his life and he felt a peace and quiet he enjoyed. He felt complete again, and the rush moved outside him, but inside he felt calm.

Perhaps the change had been too fast for them, and maybe that's why his father drank. It was his pride that was pulling him away from the family and destroying him. Lately he drank a lot with Primo, who was already coughing up cancerous blood. They were good men, but they had lost something inside and so they turned to liquor to forget that thing they once owned. And what was that thing? Pride? Honor? A need to be the undisputed leader? And why was Benjie pushing the family out of the circle of his trust? The questions tumbled like driftwood in the flowing daydream until even Roberto and Rita seemed distant, shutting themselves away from everyone as they awaited the arrival of their baby.

Finally the bell released him from the confines of the class-room, the prison as Willie called it, and Jason joined the throng of kids that swelled like a raging river through the halls and emptied into the grounds. The noise of freedom was deafening. He spotted Cristina and fought his way towards her. Usually they ate their sack lunches on the grounds, but today they had saved enough to eat at the fair and enjoy some of the rides. And this morning his mother had given him some extra money because she knew he was taking Crrstina to the fair. It never ceased to amaze him how his mother could always come up with spare change when things were so hard and tight. He had taken the money reluctantly, but he appreciated it. Someday he would pay it all back.

He had nearly reached Cristina when he heard Willie call his name. He turned and saw Willie and Chelo running towards him. "Rumble! " Willie called.

"Let's go! " Chelo shouted and grabbed his arm. Behind him he heard Cristina call his name, then she disappeared in the crowd that swept around him. He tried to tell Chelo he didn't want to go, but the momentum of the thundering torrent carried them into the street. Across the drive-in parking lot he saw the stompers running towards them, swinging belts with sharp, slashing buckles and waving jackhandles.

"Yahoo! " they shouted, "kill those mutha chucs! "

On the other side of the lot the pachucos cursed back and ran forward to meet the challenge. Their weapons were razor-sharp switchblades, brass knuckles and chains. The two sides met with a thundering clash at the confluence, like two rivers carrying different sediments they suddenly blended into one and the blood that spurted gave it its common color. The slashing buckles whizzed through the air and cut deep into tender flesh. Swishing chains broke bones and burned welts on thin skin, and the knives darted in and out like thrusting snakes. Jack handles and bats swung out and splintered brittle bones beneath hard muscle. Blows drew blood that spurted and blossomed like red flowers, and the juice of life dripped and dried on the black tar of the parking lot.

The force and savagery of the impact sent the battle crashing into the line of bystanders who had only come to watch, and they now found themselves in the middle of the melee. Girls screamed and pushed and the confusion created its own cage. Suddenly those who had only come to watch had to fight back as the blows of the fight fell on them. The pachucas joined the rumble and the stompers' girlfriends responded, and as friend joined friend to prove his loyalty the entire school population was drawn in to feed the raging madness. One brave teacher who had been nearby jumped in to part the contestants, and they turned on him and he went under.

Screams split the quiet autumn air. Handsful of hair were pulled and ripped away from tender scalp, and nails ripped through flesh and gouged at eyes. Those who went down were kicked mercilessly in the stomach and the groin, and those who remained standing were struck around the head to force them to go down. There was no safe spot; the blows landed everywhere, and in the fury of the conflict fear and safety were forgotten and the mania of survival forced its cruelty into each blow.

The vatos had not intended to fight, but once trapped and edged on by the sight of blood they too fell screaming on the stompers. Jason caught a blow from someone and went down. As he struggled to get up a hard kick ripped into his ribs and flattened him again. A big, grinning cowboy stood over him. He whirled his belt over his head and then struck. The sharp buckle came whizzing down and ripped a deep gash along Jason's cheek. At the same time Chelo struck. His blow caught the big stomper on the side of the head and knocked him down.

Chelo grabbed Jason and helped him to his feet. " ¡Vámonos a la chingada! " he shouted. Jason let Chelo lead him through the scattering crowd. Sirens had sounded and the first trio of patrol cars was already pulling into the parking lot.

"Where's Willie? " Jason shouted.

"Don't worry about him! " Chelo pulled, "He'll take care of himself! Come on! " Chelo pulled him down an alley, across a street, and they lost themselves in the alleys leading to Barelas. Squad cars were buzzing throughout the neighborhood, so they sneaked into the safety of a backyard. While they rested Chelo found a hose and washed the blood off Jason's face.

"Hurt? "

"Yeah——"

"That sonofabitch could've killed you! "

"Who was he? " Jason asked.

"His name's Darrell. He thinks he's a big chingon, but he's really an ass. He got kicked out of school years ago, for trying to rape one of the cheerleaders in the girls' gym, but he still hangs around the school. He has a truck and drinks beer all day long and keeps the rest of the little pendejitos stirred up—— But I got him good," Chelo smiled and rubbed his fist.

"Thanks," Jason nodded, "but I wish you'd a been a little faster——"

"Yeah," Chelo agreed; he frowned as he looked at the deep open wound on Jason's cheek. "Damn, I'm sorry I dragged you away——"

"Hey, it's nobody's fault," Jason interrupted him, "it just happened."

"Yeah, but if only Willie and I hadn't come by——"

Jason put his hand on Chelo's shoulder. "Come on, ése, forget it, okay. Like Pato said this morning, we can't live our lives on ifs——"

"Yeah," Chelo nodded gloomily, "at least not in Barelas . . ."

"Not anywhere," Jason added. "Hey, do you think Willie got out okay? "

"Yeah, I saw him run out when the crowd pulled back——"

"Well, we have to go back for Cristina——" Jason stood. The wound was still bleeding and soaking the handkerchief he held pressed to it.

"¿Estás loco? " Chelo argued. "You can't go back! They see you like that and they'd pick you up for sure! Hey man, don't worry about Cristina, you know she wouldn't mix up in anything like that; she's probably home by now . . ."

"But the fair——"

"Hey," Chelo smiled and put his arm around Jason as they turned down the alley, "there's not going to be any fun-time today, ése. You have to get that cut sewed up . . . Come on, let's go to Crispín's, he'll take care of you . . . With luck you'll be in shape to see Cristina tonight! "

Jason laughed weakly. "Yeah, I guess I'm not in too good a shape now . . ."

"Ah, tomorrow's another day," Chelo grinned, "the fair will still be there, the stompers will still be looking for fights, the whole chingadera'll be there . . ." They laughed and entered their barrio proudly, carrying their wounds like badges of courage.

CHAPTER TEN

Autumn had filled Barelas with its sperm-sweet smell, now the winter air licked at autumn's corners and drove the fruitful scent before it. The giant alamos of the river valley dressed in brilliant orange and invited everyone to sing the season's song, while overhead strings of geese filled the quiet, blue air with their returning call.

The river also sang, and paused as quietly as fall to watch truckloads of Corrales apples cross the bridge to find their way into the city market stalls. From Las Cruces, Belén, and Los Lunas came the vendors of chile verde and maíz, and from Isleta Pueblo the Indians brought sheep, ristras de chile, and blue corn meal. The barrio paused to buy; the winter would be long.

. . . Overhead the golden deer ran south, fleeing the cold winter storms of the north. Trails of his golden sperm turned the mountains red and gold . . .

In Barelas the air was sweet and heavy with the fragrance of burning leaves, the smell of roasting chile verde, and the soft call of lovers. The earth gave up her fruit and rested. Rita brought her baby into the light of the world and rested. The feast of the baptism was prepared.

La fiesta del bautismo, it was an ancient custom. Padrinos were chosen, godparents who would instruct the child and take an active interest in his life. In this way, also, the family was expanded, and it grew to include los compadres. It was insurance for the new born baby, not insurance bought on paper for money, but an assurance that there would always be someone in the community to whom the growing child could turn; it was a reaffirmation of faith in the community of people. Early in the morning the padrinos came for the baby and took it to church to be baptised by the priest who would christen the baby and annoint him with holy water. That was also a part of the ritual, but the most meaningful part was when the baby was returned and he was baptized by the love of the people.

Roberto was proud. Friends and neighbors filled his small home, he drank with everyone, his abrazos were for all. It was his first child, and the good birth presaged many more. He beamed as he passed out cigars and kept everyone's glass full. Toast after toast rocked the small house as the baby was passed from arms to arms. Everyone admired the new born son. The women cuddled him and pointed out his handsome features.

"——Such beautiful brown eyes! "

"Oh, he will be dark and handsome, I could hold him forever! "

"No le vayan a hacer mal ojo," the madrina said and guarded her new care jealously, and she took the baby and gave it to Dorotea, old Manuel's wife, so that she might shield the baby from the admiring and piercing glances which could set the evil eye. And Dorotea received the baby and sat in a quiet corner of the house to cradle and comfort the child, and she fell in love with the new, smiling son. Her withered breasts ached to nurse a child again.

The men also admired the child, but they showed their admiration by predicting how the child would fulfill his destiny.

"He has big hands, strong hands," old Manuel laughed, "I will teach him to be a woodcutter like me! "

Another spoke up. "He has bright eyes, that means intelligence. He will be a lawyer or a teacher——"

"Strong hands to hold a gun," Lalo cut in unexpectedly, "and clear eyes to see the injustices being done to the people! " Then because the men did not respond he stalked away gloomily.

"No, no, no," Primo shook his head, "he has strong shoulders and a strong back. He will work in the shops like his father."

"No! " Roberto spoke for the first time, "I do not want my son to work in the shops, I do not want him to follow in my footsteps." He looked lovingly at his son and said, "I want him to have an education——" He felt the silence he had created and he looked at the chorus of men that would pass judgement on what he said, and he looked down and finished speaking his thoughts. "Work in the shops is good for us who are strong and don't know anything else, and it is good for a son to follow in his father's footsteps and do the work his father did. That is the way it has always been. But I have a different dream for my son. I want him to have an education! " he said emphatically. "That's the only way he can free himself and be what he wants to be—— I know we have a lot of good things here in the barrio, and we are fortunate to have good friends and neighbors, but there are also a lot of things we don't have. It is important that we educate our sons to go out and see the world and learn the things we didn't learn——" His voice was full of emotion. He knew he was pleading his case before his peers.

"In Korea, those of us that didn't have an education froze and died on the front lines, I learned that. We didn't complain because we had the courage and the honor to do it, but it doesn't always have to be that way. The only way to change those things is to begin to study them and understand them, and that is why I plan as I do for my son. In the shops, we do the hard, back-breaking work, we haul the city's garbage, and we are the ones that have to move constantly in search of work. I don't believe it has to be this way. I believe in revolution, like Lalo believes in revolution, but I think the revolution will be done by educating our children. Later, they will return to help us, in their own way they will return to work for our good. I trust in that. Now all I can do is teach him to be free to know himself, teach him that he has a strong will, like papá taught us to be proud." He finished what he had to say and he glanced at his father.

The room was silent. The men did not look at each other, because today they would not pass judgement. Many of them felt like Roberto and they knew he had been eloquent in his statement, but they did not yet understand the far-reaching consequences of this revolution Roberto spoke about. In the back of each man's mind there lingered the question: Would it destroy their way of life? They had seen other educated and successful men stray away from the community.

"Education for your son is a fine thing," an elderly man spoke, "we have always encouraged it for our children. But what of those who learn and go away, of what good are they to the people? How do they serve the people? " The rest of the men nodded.

"Not my son," Roberto insisted, "he will return to work for his people! "

101

"It is true! " Clemente jumped up, "Perhaps this is the leader we have waited for! A man for the people! " He grabbed the baby from Dorotea's lap and held him up for everyone to see.

The men nodded in agreement. Perhaps the new child would be a leader, didn't each new birth contain such a promise? Wasn't this the reason that each birth brought a breath of fresh hope to their struggle? The times called for a strong and fearless leader.

"My son! " Rita cried and reached for her baby, but Clemente reeled around the room, holding the baby aloft.

"My precious one! " Dorotea also clutched for the baby, but she could not reach him.

"A born leader! A born leader! " Clemente cried drunkenly, and he laughed and spun around the room. The women cried out, fearing that he would drop the baby, but Clemente reeled to a stop in front of Crispín.

"Crispín, old friend, it is rumored that you have the power to see into a man's future! Tell us, is this the Chávez that will lead the people to the rightful place in their land? "

The crowd grew still. They knew of Crispín's powers, so their expectancy charged the room with tension. They waited.

Crispín drew close to Clemente and his blind eyes were like a mirror. Then he touched Clemente's shoulder and whispered, "It is true, this Chávez will lead——"

Clemente recoiled at the words. For a moment he thought he had seen himself in the blind man's eyes. The old man's words rang in his ears with frightening clarity. He turned away to hide his emotion and at the same time Dorotea reached out and grabbed the baby. The other women shrieked and applauded. They gathered around the baby and made over him. The men roared with laughter.

"Your grandson is going to lead the women out of the kitchen! " Old Manuel joked and fed the laughter.

"——Bendito entre todas las mujeres," Primo added.

Clemente turned away. He reached for a drink to calm his trembling. From where he stood he stole a glance at the blind prophet's eyes, seeking to decipher the strange message that had cut through his heart. What did the old man mean, and why did Crispín's words make him shake like a leaf?

"To be a leader a man must know the traditions of his father, and I am afraid this new generation knows nothing of the old ways," one of the old men said softly. "All they seem to be interested in is that loud be-bop music and smoking that devil's weed, marijuana. The boys waste their time chasing girls and drinking, and combing their hair. It is a generation of the city, and it is a lost generation. I know, I have lived long enough to see it. In the city we have forgotten the old ways,· and we have changed until we have become like the gringo. God pity us, but it is true——"

"La crianza was in the land," another added, "the earth was like a mother that provided us everything we needed. Oh, it was not always easy, there were many long, cold winters and periods of drought, but we kept our faith because the earth taught us that faith of renewal. The seasons changed, and the earth changed, and we understood our role in those cycles. We knew the directions of the wind, and when an ill wind brought poor times or tragedy we pitched in and helped each other, and when there were good times we rejoiced."

"It is true," his friend nodded, "the communal life of the pueblo or the ranchito supported each person. And the life of the village was reflected in the spirit of la familia. We didn't need welfare, we helped each other; and our old people were not put in nursing homes, they occupied a role of respect in la familia. Times are changing, now every man seems isolated, every man cares only for his own good——"

"How did all this happen? " A young man asked. He had been listening intently to the stories.

"Because we lost the land," one of the men answered. "A new way of life and a new set of laws pushed us out of the land grants. We lost las mercedes and the communal lands——"

"We were dispersed from our own land, our way of life was destroyed, we had to recreate our pueblos in the slum-barrios of the cities! "

The men grew angry and bitter when they talked about the lost land.

They told stories about the deeding of the land grants and the history behind the families who settled throughout the territory, and most important, they told in detail the aspects of the daily life of the people. And in the end they told how the government and men of power using the new laws for selfish gain encroached upon the land and finally wrenched it away.

"——And now? "

"And now," the old man laughed, "we are gatherings of old and feeble men and women, living in memories of a time past, but we still have the strength to fight this government for what is rightfully ours. We must regain the land, and we must teach our children that spiritual attachment to the earth, because——" He paused and looked at the children who listened. "There is no other redeemer than our mother earth. Remember that. Only the earth can redeem our humanity, only she can renew our faith." He turned to the other men and said, "I shudder to think that as my sons know only the cement and asphalt of the city, so their hearts may become hard and cold like concrete——"

The men nodded in agreement, then the conversation drifted to other topics. The feast continued, the laughter of enjoyment rocked the small house, and the last guests left very late. They left behind them a good feeling of sharing. The curse of the evil eye that was also left was not done with intention or with malice, it was only that admiring eyes looked too closely at the baby's soul and drew it out.

That night the baby became ill. Rita called Adelita and they gave the baby an enema, and then a little bit of water flavored with osha to drink. But nothing they tried would comfort him. He continued to cry and to throw up everything they tried to feed him. He grew limp and pale from crying and coughing.

"We must call the doctor! " Rita finally cried in desperation, and Roberto went across the street to use Manuel's telephone. He came back with bad news. No doctor would come to the barrio at that late hour of the night.

"They all say wait until morning and then take him to the clinic," Roberto shrugged with exasperation.

"We can't wait! " Rita cried hysterically, "My baby is sick! He might die——" she sobbed.

"No, mi'ja, do not think like that," Adelita tried to comfort her, but she too felt defeated. She had tried every remedy she knew but the baby continued vomiting, and his strong cries had changed to gasps for air. They would have to do something immediately.

"We must take him to the hospital! "

"Yes——"

"To the hospital? " The dark figure at the door interrupted them. "Take my precious one to the hospital! Oh, nooo——" It was Dorotea. She had heard Roberto telephone the doctor, and suspecting what had happened she followed him. She grinned and picked up the sick child. She looked carefully at the baby, felt its stomach and tested for empache.

"Oh, pobrecito," she shook her head, "it is just as I thought——"

"What? " Rita cried.

"El mal de ojo," Dorotea whispered and rolled her eyes. "Someone has given your baby the evil eye——"

" ¡El mal de ojo! " Rita gasped, "But who? "

Dorotea smiled. "Whoever admired your child the most today," she answered.

"But that was everyone here! " Rita exclaimed.

"——And only the person who laid el mal de ojo can cure it," Dorotea shook her head wisely, "and that person must be found before a Friday passes, or else——"

"I don't believe in those things," Roberto scoffed. "We will take my son to the hospital! "

"Bah! What does the gringo doctor know! " Dorotea cried angrily. "And who asked you to believe, huh! I will cure this baby——"

"But Dorotea," Adelita asked, "if you can cure the baby that means that it was you who set the evil eye? "

Dorotea hung her head. "Soy de sangre pesada," she said timidly, "and I have been known to cause the sores on sick people to boil and ache. But let us not waste anytime. You! " She turned to Roberto, "go to the kitchen and have some coffee while I take care of things here! It does not help to have a pendejo around when one works the remedies of faith. Adelita, bring me some holy water, and two fresh eggs——"

She undressed the baby and when Adelita returned with the jar of holy water the old woman filled her mouth with the water and then held her lips to the baby and made him drink. She also spit forcefully on the baby's forehead. Then to insure a double remedy she rubbed the baby with the cold water of the church. She also broke one of the eggs and rubbed the baby's back and stomach with the white of the egg. When she was finished she wrapped the baby in a clean blanket and handed him to Rita. Rita gathered the limp bundle in her arms. She pressed her child to her bosom and felt his cool forehead. He was asleep already, resting for the first time that night.

"Perhaps it was me," Dorotea shook her head and prepared to leave, "ah, well, they say adoration is envy's sister. Tomorrow I will bring the baby a present of red coral to protect it from other eyes——" She gathered her black shawl around her shoulders and went out laughing.

"I can't believe it," Rita murmured, "but I am thankful." She opened her blouse and let her hungry child nurse.

"No harm was meant," Adelita shivered and closed the door. Tomorrow would be Friday.

CHAPTER ELEVEN

Both life and death came to the barrio. Like twin brothers in the wind-stream of the universe the current swept down and whispered a cold fall song. A full November moon rose over the Sandías and sought its reflection in the deep waters of the canal that ran along the river. White and round and disrobed, the moon rose like a woman after summer love, her silver fingers pulling at the waters of the earth. Old women muttered strange warnings and pulled the window curtains so that the cold light would not fall upon their daughters as they slept.

It was a deer moon, sister of the sleeping sun, she bathed the earth and moved along his ancient summer path . . .

On Barelas road Jason and Chelo paused as they saw the huge golden moon disentangle herself from the bare elm tree branches to move above them.

"Damn that's a big moon! " Chelo exclaimed.

"A deer moon . . ." Jason whispered. Chelo was about to ask him what he meant when suddenly Henry rushed at them. He was upon them like an animal, grunting and growling and picking up dirt from the street to fling at them. Chelo cried in terror and fell back. Then they recognized the dark, naked form that had confronted them so suddenly.

"It's Henry! " Jason shouted.

"He's gotten loose! We better get Willie! "

"Henry! " Jason shouted and stood in his way to try to stop him, but Henry easily slipped around him. "Grab him! " Jason shouted at Chelo. Chelo lunged at Henry and tackled him, but he couldn't hold on. Henry easily broke Chelo's grip then picked him up and threw him on the ground. Before Jason could move in he scampered away, laughing and flinging dirt at them.

"Damn!" Chelo groaned as Jason helped him up, "I didn't

know he was that strong! Did you see the way he picked me up, like I was nothing——"

"He's headed for la 'cequia! " Jason pointed.

"He always heads for the water——" Chelo dusted himself. Henry's strength had surprised and frightened him more than the fall had hurt him.

"Yaaa-ooooooow-hee-heeeeeee——" Henry's shrill cry wound down the dark alley, like the cry of the returning son answering the wail of la Llorona. But tonight it was the full golden moon that hung on the elm tree branches that made Henry run and leap with joy.

"Loooooooo-nah! " His call echoed out of the darkness.

The dogs of the barrio returned his cry, but they did not move out to challenge the dark intruder.

"We gotta get Rufus and Willie——"

"There's no time! He's headed for the water! "

" ¡Vamos! "

Without hesitation they followed Henry into the dark corner of the barrio and along the rutty paths that led to the irrigation canal. The sharp, dry grass of the alkaline flats crunched beneath their feet, and the giant alamos that had lost their bark stood like spectre sentries at the gateway of darkness. The night air was damp and misty. Birds screeched in the tree tops as they fluttered awake to the noise of the chase.

They lost him in the heavy brush. They followed every rustling sound they heard until they too were lost in the thicket. When they stopped to listen for him all they could hear were their pounding hearts and gasps for breath. Chelo suggested they go back, and when they turned they came upon the clearing by the stream where Clemente had witnessed the primal dance months before. There stood Henry. He was naked, poised at the edge of the dark water. His sweating chest heaved and glistened in the moonlight. He had finished his dance to the moon; tonight his possession of her would be complete.

"Luna . . ." he whispered and raised his arms to the full, golden orb. This was his dream, to touch the shining, oval face. This was his only love. He had already danced for her at the water's edge, and now she called to him from where she glistened on the smooth surface of her watery bed.

"Luna . . ." he called lovingly and stepped softly into the icy water. He laughed with joy as he reached out and touched the golden water. Always before the giant bear had come to take him away from the light he yearned for, but tonight he was alone. The golden arms of the moon embraced him and he scooped the water and drank.

"He's calling the moon! " Jason gasped, and suddenly he knew why Henry had always run to the water of la'cequia.

"He's crazy! " Chelo shouted as they ran to the edge of the bank. "Hennnnn-rrrry! " He cried.

Henry paused and turned. Tonight they were not going to rob him of the light he loved. He turned and moved quickly towards the middle of the dark stream. The moon was like a mermaid resting on the flowing water, singing and calling to him. He reached out and gathered the moonbeams resting on the surface of the water and drank them. His dark fingers ripped open the water and the moonlight rippled away like sparkling diamonds. The reflection was always just ahead of him, drawing him on.

He was up to his chest, still laughing. He reached for the light and it shattered into dozens of smaller moons, and he played with and teased the children of his mother. He drank the light on the water until he could drink no more, until he could breathe it in no more. Then suddenly the deceptive current clutched at his legs and drew him under.

"He's gone down! " Chelo shouted. They ran along the bank, trying to keep in sight the dark figure that tumbled over and over in the deep water.

"We gotta go in for him! " Jason answered. He stopped and stripped away his jacket.

"No! " Chelo protested vigorously, "You can't! He's too strong, he'll drown you! "

"I've got to! " Jason cried, "He'll drown——" He kicked away his shoes and turned to dive into the cold, churning water.

"No! " Chelo grabbed him and wrestled him to the ground. "He'll drown you! " Chelo shouted as they tumbled on the bank, "He's too strong! If he grabs you he'll take you under! "

"Let go! " Jason cried and struggled to get loose, but Chelo's bearhug was too strong to break. And while they struggled on the sandy bank Henry slipped into a swirling whirlpool. Instead of fighting the grip of the water he laughed and went on reaching for the diamond glitter of the light. The gurgling vortex drew him down three times and each time he went down Henry drank the golden beams that filtered through the water. The last time he surfaced he saw the golden moon hanging in the sky and he smiled his last goodbye, then his lungs burst and he went down to surface no more. So it was the moon that stole away his soul and not the cold waters that drowned him, and he tumbled in the dark waters as if playing in the freedom of the light which had released him.

Jason finally broke Chelo's hold. He scrambled to the edge of the roaring waters and shouted into the tempest that thundered at his ears:

"Hen-riiieeeee! "

But Henry was gone; he tumbled in his shroud of water and entered the fish-thumping river, and the river gathered him in its arms and pulled him south towards the sea.

Chelo and Jason ran along the bank, looking for the body. They ran as far as the Barelas Bridge, and there they fell exhausted on the sandy bank. The search was useless, Henry was gone.

"It's cold," Chelo shivered. They were sweating, and now the cold night air chilled them.

"I can't see anything in this damned darkness! " Jason shouted in exasperation. He felt empty inside, helpless in the face of death.

They both felt they had lost something. The summers in Barelas would not be complete without Henry sitting on the Army cot beneath the elm tree to which he was chained. He was gone now, and a part of what he had been to them was ripped away from their insides and drowned in the stream. They looked around and found themselves alone, and they cursed because they felt that all of Barelas should come running to the water's edge to grieve for Henry. Even the moon shrouded herself in a dark cloud and mourned.

But nothing changed.

The cars crept slowly across the narrow Barelas Bridge. Somewhere a screen door banged shut, and someone shouted to a friend, "Hey, man, I'm ready. Let's go! "

Nothing changed.

"I had to stop you," Chelo muttered, trying to explain the loss and impotency he felt.

"I know," Jason nodded.

"He was too strong for us. When he picked me up back there in the street, I felt how strong he was. I was afraid, because I have never felt strength like that before. I knew that if he grabbed hold of you he would have drowned you with him——"

Jason stood up. He looked down the stream of shimmering water. "We gotta go tell Rufus, and Willie——"

"Yeah."

Jason shrugged. "Que chinga."

CHAPTER TWELVE

The sun sucked the holy waters of the river, and the turtle-bowl sky ripped open with dark thunder and fell upon the land. South of Aztlán the golden deer drank his fill and tasted the sweet fragrance of the drowned man's blood. That evening he bedded down with the turtle's sisters and streaked their virgin robes with virgin blood.

Oh, wash my song into the dead man's soul, he cried, and soak his marrow dry. Let his eyes burst like dying suns, and let his blood sweeten my fields of corn . . .

The deep water of the canal had dumped Henry in the river, and the muddy current of the fish-thumping river sang as it enveloped its burden. It was a high river that bore the body southward, towards the land of the sun, beyond succor, past the last blessing of las cruces, into the dissolution that lay beyond el paso de la muerte. Dams could not stop the body that rolled and turned like a golden fish returning to its home. It was not until the body found a quiet pool that the wires of a jetty could reach out like death's fingers and tangle the body in their grasp. Now the cold waters rumbled with the same insanity which had once driven Henry. The moon waned and loosened its grip upon the sea. The river churned then ebbed. The sun brought out an innocent fisherman who cast his hook and snagged dead Henry's heart.

"I'm telling you, you can't open that casket! " The county coroner insisted. He shifted his cigar in his mouth and placed his hands on his hips. He stood between Rufus and the casket he had just delivered to the mortuary door. He was a big man and he knew the law, and the law said to get rid of the remains as soon as possible. "Why, man, there's more water wrapped in that plastic bag in the casket then there is body——" He shook his head.

"My son has been returned to us for a purpose," Rufus answered calmly. "He must have a proper velorio. It is our custom to have a wake for the dead——" He looked at Montoya who stood nervously by the casket.

"I have nothing to do with this——" Montoya wrung his hands. When he heard Rufus was coming to claim the body he had called the priest. Now he turned for support to father Cayo.

"I know how you feel," the priest said to Rufus, "but things being as they are why don't we just say a rosary for the dearly departed, and have the coroner bury him. The county has jurisdiction in these matters——"

"You will not pray at his velorio? " Rufus asked.

"Impossible! " The priest shook his head and turned away.

"Then I have no use for you," Rufus shrugged. "I will take my son home. There the living will view the dead, the rosary will be prayed, the alabados will be sung. The velorio will last all night as is prescribed by custom; the body will not be left alone. Then in the morning he can be buried—— It is the proper thing to do, it's all I have to give him——"

As he moved toward the casket he remembered the death of his mother. Her eyes had not closed, and his father in his grief had placed two Liberty half dollars on her eyelids. It was the last human touch she felt while on earth, he remembered that. When they were ready to seal the casket the half dollars were removed and the eyes remained closed. It was then he understood death and he was able to cry. His father had given him the silver and he had carried them with him since. Now he had to see his son's eyes, he had to be sure that death would let them close in peace. He wanted to give his son the silver pieces blessed by his mother so long ago. It would be his last remembrance.

"You cannot move this body without proper authorization! " The coroner blocked his way. In one swift movement Rufus thrust him aside.

"I will take my son home," Rufus said sternly. He nodded and Willie helped him slip the plain, welfare casket on his back. He bent like a mule and grunted, but he lifted the heavy load. He trudged away from Montoya's Mortuary bearing the crushing load to his simple home.

It was a strange procession that followed him down the winding streets of the barrio. The news spread ahead of the slow cortege and people came to their gates to see the dog-killer Christ bearing his cross. Behind him trudged his insane wife, her black shawl pulled around her head to hide her face from staring eyes. Her children followed, frightened and cringing, bewildered by the world beyond their home. Some of the old women of the barrio pulled their black shawls over their heads and left what they were doing to follow the mournful procession. One began to pray the rosary, and the refrain of Hail Marys from the chorus mixed into the dust of the street and rose into the bright light of the afternoon.

Crispín came, and he strummed his guitar softly. A sad dirge for poor, dead Henry.

Rufus did not look back. He moved ahead with a determination that would not be deterred. Once he tripped and an old man stepped forward to help him. When they had straightened the heavy casket on his back, Rufus thanked the man and continued on. They understood his need to bear the weight alone. They did not speak, but their presence was a strength. When the slow, arduous march neared the house some of the men went ahead to set some crates on which to rest the casket, then they helped Rufus place the back-breaking load on that simple resting place. He wanted to be alone with his dead son, and so the mourners waited outside while Rufus took a crowbar and opened the coffin.

The plain lid snapped open and the smell of death permeated the room. Rufus did not recognize the remains, but still a quiet sadness made him sigh. He wanted to pray, but he couldn't find the right words. Instead he opened the plastic bag and placed the two half dollars on the sunken pits that were once Henry's eyes. Rufus smiled. His son would have two golden moons to light his way into eternity. He crossed his forehead and then sealed everything as it had been.

The women of the barrio entered and cleaned the cluttered house while Rufus and his wife sat quietly beside the coffin. They opened the windows and aired the house, and they lit a candle at the foot of the coffin and burned incense to drive away the bad smell of death. One woman brought a bouquet of roses and set

114

them on the coffin. The house was swept clean and the kitchen was scrubbed so the feast of the wake could be prepared. The children of Rufus looked bewildered, but the tenderness of the women drew them out of their isolation and soon they too were helping.

The women worked cheerfully as they prepared the food for the velorio. It was custom that there should be plenty of food for the mourners who came to keep the vigil of the wake at night, so everyone helped and contributed something. So the storehouse of food grew in the kitchen. Nimble fingers pressed the round tortillas that became the bread of the wake. Pots of beans were brought and their rich fragrance blended into the aroma of the roasting chile verde. The mourners also brought other gifts of food. An old friend from Belén brought a goat which he butchered in the back yard, and soon there was tender carne de cabrito roasting in the oven. In Los Padillas the blood of a lamb was saved and made into a rich blood pudding which became the gift that was offered with el pésame to Rufus and his wife. Bowls of carne adovada, skillets of red chile de riztra made by hand, and pastelitos made of dried fruit also were brought until the tables in the kitchen were heaped high with food for the mourners. Wine and whiskey were also delivered so that there would be plenty of drink to wet the parched throats that prayed and sang for Henry's place in heaven.

Black coffee brewed on the stove, and its fragrance and the sweet scent of the burning piñon wood wafted into the living room and roused Rufus from his thoughts. He looked around and saw his neighbors, and what they were doing for him brought tears to his eyes. He smiled and understood that tomorrow he would be Rufus the dog killer again, and that the children of the barrio would taunt him as he scavenged in the alleys, and they would sing songs about his insane wife. Tomorrow he would withdraw once again into the shell of his solitude, and he would walk the streets of Barelas not with the weight of his son's coffin on his back but with the burden of his loneliness. He could accept that, because what had happened today would make that easier to bear.

Evening came and the mourners filled the small house. Then the man who would sing the alabados arrived. His name was Lázaro, and he was tall and gaunt, like an old, giant, gnarled alamo.

Wrapped in his dusty, World War One coat, he looked like an old prophet walking out of the pages of the Bible, out of place in a world which called itself modern, he scoffed at time because his soul was timeless and intact. He towered over the children that gathered outside the house and the power of his one good eye made them cringe and part to let him pass. He was tattered and unshaven, and some laughed at the long hair that fell like a lion's mane around his shoulders, but he had a gift, and that was that he could sing the old prayers and make God cry in heaven.

With his long duster-coat flowing behind him he walked quickly to the foot of the coffin and he cried out, " ¡Arrímense vivos y difuntos, aquí estamos todos juntos! " His voice cracked with the essence of prayer and brought the mourners to their knees.

" ¡Oyeme Dios! " He raised his hands toward heaven and called upon the Lord to hear him. The people bowed their heads and waited for the earth to shake.

" ¡La voz de Dios habla por el espíritu humano, y no hay muerte en este mundo! " He cried out.

"Alabados sean los dulces nombres," the women responded and made the sign of the cross. None dared look up at this man who called upon the spirit of God as a companion and a friend to be with them that night.

"Hear me, Father! " One-eyed Lázaro sang, "I have come to sing the prayers for the dead——" His voice rose sonorously in the smoke of the burning candles. "I will sit by the throne of the Lord and sing my songs for my dead brother——" He carried all of the old alabados in his heart, and he was sure that they would please the Lord. He had walked in God's path all of his life, he had renounced the world and its goods, he had walked through the door of death from an old life into a new one and so he knew that God listened to him. He was a man who conversed with God, a holy man, a man who had not sinned. And when he felt God turn to listen he threw himself on the floor and knelt before the coffin.

"Padre nuestro que'stas en los cielos, santificado sea tu nombre——" He began his prayers. This was his prayer to the Lord, the opening lines of the drama he would re-create this night. He would sing to God and lead the chorus of women through the dark journey of the long night until they felt the presence of death and the power of God. He would drive the knowledge of death into

116

their hearts.

"Pray for us sinners, now and at the hour of our death . . ." The women answered the dolorous sound of Lázaro's dry voice.

He rocked on his knees and made them understand that the body itself is a coffin, and the spirit is entombed in its blood-dark flesh. He made them understand that Henry's entrapment in the dark coffin was like theirs. His dry, raspy voice in measured meter sought to draw them into the confines of the coffin so that they could feel the presence of death.

Some of the men rose to stretch and to go outside to urinate against the side of the house, but the women did not leave the one-eyed prophet. His high, quavering voice took them from hymn to hymn. It faltered at times and broke the rhythm, but it never descended from the hypnotic tempo that drove them higher and higher towards a climax with death. The concentric rings of mourners became one. The flickering light of the burning candles blurred in their eyes and reminded them of the brevity of life, and the coffin made them fear eternity. The immense weight of the mystery of death and un-ending time pressed down on them, and relief was only within the meaning in the dark coffin.

The rest of the men got up and left off praying, moving quietly into the kitchen for a cigarette and a drink, but the women remained. Children fell asleep as Lázaro reached into his vast storehouse of songs and prayers to continue the velorio, to continue the wake that became a vigil and a conversation with one's soul. Finally the sing-song of the alabados, the fatigue, the incense of the burning candles, and the essence of faith raised the mourners to a climax where all emotions became one. There was union with the rotting flesh in the sealed casket, and the illusion of life fell away like a veil as they made the connection with death and its eternity. Suddenly the immense weight was lifted. The woman nearest the coffin cried out, "¡Dios mío! ¡Dios mío! " She clutched at the casket and tried to rip away the covering. Like the others, she had been driven to a vision of eternity, and she was engulfed with pity for dead Henry.

The other women reached out to help her. A flood of tears broke loose and they cried. Relief found its way into their tired bodies. They sighed and rested their souls. They comforted each other.

117

Lázaro rose and went to the kitchen. His legs felt stiff, and there was an empty feeling in his stomach. God had listened, he knew, and God had heard him. The prayers of the women were sweet to God and he had shown them the path that Henry would walk; and they understood that eventually they all walked in that timeless void. The Lord is good, Lázaro thought. One of the men handed him a bottle and he took a drink.

"Gracias," he acknowledge the drink. "What time is it? "

"Past twelve, compadre," the man answered. "You prayed four hours straight——"

"Now we must eat," he said before he went outside for a breath of fresh air, "then we must pray again. We must pray until the lucero of dawn appears in the sky——"

They would keep the vigil of the dead until the rosy fingers of dawn reached over the Sandía Mountain and bathed the barrio with·the yellow light of the new day. They would alternate praying with eating. Bottles of wine and tequilla and whiskey would be emptied, and the kitchen would roar and shake with laughter. Old stories would be told, gossip would be exchanged, and the merriment and gusto of the feast of the dead would alternate with the time for praying. Lázaro's songs and prayers would heighten their awareness of death, so they would celebrate the brevity of life. That is what the velorio was about.

It re-enacted the mystery of Christ and the mystery of every life. Each man was born, he lived and died, and he rose again into the mysterious whispering winds of the universe. So the velorio was not a period to life, nor a gathering to praise the end, but rather a reaffirmation of a simple, common humanity which they all shared.

CHAPTER THIRTEEN

A long, cold winter settled over Barelas. The lines grew long at the welfare door where meager commodities were doled out to the people. Men stood with their faces downcast, ashamed to face their neighbors. Each collected his gunny sack full of rice, corn meal, powdered milk and rancid butter, then he hurried away to a cold home. It was a harsh winter, with nearly half of the men of Barelas out of work.

Many families moved back to the small villages, but there was little left there. At least there were old roots of the family to return to, those who had not succumbed to the lure of the city. They welcomed back their wandering kin and made room to accommodate them for the winter. They gathered around the wood-burning stoves and caught up on the news of the family and old neighbors:

Epifano moved his family to California . . .

Clory's boy, the one you used to call el mocoso, he was killed in a car accident by Las Animas . . .

Jesús Sena passed by here, on his way north to the beet fields of Colorado . . .

You remember don Amadeo, the old man who used to deliver goat milk, he died. They say somebody put a curse on him. He used to live like a hermit, but when they went to his hut they found thousands of dollars hidden all over the place . . .

And you remember Julia, she went to high school with your Josephine. Her family used to live in that big house by la mesita, right where the road turned. Yes, her father was a compadre to my tío Alfredo, they had been friends for years before they quarreled over some cows that had trampled my tío Alfredo's corn field. That man shot my uncle, that's how he lost his leg. Anyway, she married Arturo Sandoval, he's from Vallecito, although that family was originally from Bernalillo. He had run for county sheriff and lost and after that he got thrown in jail every weekend, for drinking, by the man who won. Well, he had been married before, and anyway, he was too old for her, and so she started seeing the young man who came to cut wood for them. You remember him, he was with that bunch of boys that . . .

And it went on and on, a reweaving of the family histories, a catching up on the events that formed the total fabric of the community. It was important to keep track of relatives as they spread out across the land, it was important to tell the young the names of cousins they had in far-away places so that if they ever traveled in those lands they would know their family blood, and tragedies might be averted.

Those that remained in Barelas continued their enslavement in the shops. At least it was work, but because so many men had been fired or laid-off the work crews were small and each man had to do the work of two. Accidents occured daily. Stiff, frozen hands that did not move fast enough lost fingers, eyes went blind from sudden, careless explosions, sharp steel slashed at arms and legs, and everywhere bits of flesh clung to the searing-cold steel. The enslavement became final when each man withdrew into himself and was concerned only with his own individual survival. Lalo and his small band of strikers kept up their efforts, but their call for unity was like a child's whimper lost in the winds of winter.

In the desolate winter evenings the dark figures of men trudged across the black snow, seeking the warmth and safety of home. By sunset the barrio streets were deserted. The pulse of life that throbbed so vibrantly in the summer now seemed dead and grieved by the cold winds that buffeted the barrio. The storms moved farther south than usual that winter, and the cold froze the desert land until the earth herself seemed to forget her promise of life.

Long after the last of the men had moved across the frozen wasteland, one solitary figure lurched down the wind-swept street. It was Clemente Chávez. He leaned into the swirling wind of the blizzard, but the force of the storm was too strong and he was too

120

weakened by alcohol to fight it. He tripped and fell into the gutter. He made an effort to rise but he could not, and then because he already felt his spirit was dead he lay still and let his body lie in the cold snow. The snow drifted around him and began to cover him, and he greeted it. It was like the wine he drank, one more veil covering the consciousness he wanted buried. He renounced life and did not struggle.

He reviewed his life and found that it no longer had meaning, and wasn't this, after all, the logical end of his drinking? Wasn't the door of death his wish? There was no reason to go on living. He could not survive on the welfare line, and he could not live without his honor and pride. All that was gone, he had lost it somewhere in the past, perhaps with the first drink he had taken months ago. He had lost his land and his family, and nothing else really mattered. He smiled and welcomed death.

The cold spread over him and stiffened his limbs. The images of his past flowed through his mind as death settled over him. Before he passed into unconsciousness he saw himself as a young man, riding across the sunlit llano to arrive home before the sunset. He felt the horse strong and powerful under him. Horse and man were one, a jubilant surge of energy in rhythm to the sun and the turning earth. He smiled and sang as he thundered across the plain. Then he heard someone call his name and he thought he saw the face of his father.

He struggled to open black, frozen lips to answer the call of his father.

"¡Clemente! " The voice called again, and warm fingers touched his frozen face. Clemente's frozen eyelids fluttered open.

"Crispín——" He smiled weakly, "old friend, my time has come——"

Crispín shook his head. "No, there is no death here——"

"I welcome death——" Clemente moaned.

"A man cannot find death if death is not looking for that man," Crispín said. "I tell you, if death were here you could see him sitting at your left side; he would talk to you like a brother . . . Instead there is an old man at your side, a blind man who could not sleep because the wind of the storm whispered that he should come to this place . . . Come, it is time to go." He placed his arm under Clemente and with a heave he lifted the frozen body.

121

It was an act of faith which gave him the strength to carry Clemente down the dark streets of Barelas through the blinding, sweeping snow. The frail musician's back strained under the weight of despair which he carried through the storm, but he did not falter. Within himself he knew why the vision had called him into the winter night. Three times he stumbled but each time his resolution overcame the fury of the storm. The vision had called him to fulfill a purpose and now the same source lent him the inner strength to deliver Clemente to warmth and safety. He laid Clemente on the bed and rubbed life back into the cold limbs. When Clemente could sit up Crisín held a cup of hot, strong coffee to his lips, and then he lit a cigarette for him.

"Gracias," Clemente muttered. He was still shaking from the cold, but he felt life returning. The taste of good coffee and the pleasant smoke of the cigarette made him realize how close he had been to death. "And now? " he asked Crispín.

"From death a man can only walk into life," Crispín answered.

"But why? Why? " Clemente groaned.

"To begin a new search, a new journey," Crispín's voice rang clear, and because it reached the roots of Clemente's soul it drew out the agonizing question Clemente had avoided for so long.

"— —To search for the heart of Aztlán? " He asked in a quivering voice. "How do I know I am the man? "

"You will never know if you do not search," Crispín replied.

Clemente trembled with despair and doubt. "But where will I find this place? " He asked. "How will I know the way? "

"There are signs," Crispín whispered, "a man only has to search for the signs, they are all around him! "

. . . *In the ancient legends there was a white, burning desert through which the sacred river ran, and to the east in the direction of the life-giving sun there was the magic mountain. There in that wilderness are the ruins of Aztlán; there in that sacred mountain is the fountain of Aztlán, the source of the river of our people . . .*

"— —It is true," Clemente's body convulsed as he let the truth seep through him, "I must begin that search. That is why I was spared tonight— —" For the first time in months he felt there was purpose to his life.

"¡Por Dios Santo! " He exclaimed, "That is what I need to live! " I will search for those signs, I will find that magic heart of our land about which you whisper, and I will wrestle from it the holy power to help my people! " He laughed and cried with joy. "I don't know if this is an insanity that possesses me, but at least it has a purpose. I feel that purpose! " He cried and reached out and grabbed Crispín's shoulders to communicate his feelings.

"Good," Crispín smiled. "So the storm tonight was your baptism——" He poured hot coffee from the pot on the small, wood-burning stove. "Where will you begin? " He asked.

Clemente thought awhile. "They say a journey always begins at home," he mused, "so why don't I start with you, old friend. You are a far wiser man than I, and you know the legend of Aztlán——"

"So you want to hear the story," Crispín nodded. He picked up the blue guitar and strummed the magic strings.

"There are many versions of the legend of Aztlán," Crispín began. "It is said that *the people* were the first human beings to walk on the shores of Aztlán. Where they came from is not recorded in the annals of the sun, and the stories have been so eroded by the waters of the stream of time that only a sentence or two remain to give an intimation of the entire story. Some say *the people* were a wandering tribe of the ancient world, spared during the drowning of the earth so that they might establish a civilization of peace in the new world. Other versions go further back and say that Aztlán was a floating continent that settled north of Mexico when the earth was young. There are seven springs on the sacred mountain, and the Indians call this the sipapu, the place of origin. The rays of the sun penetrated the dark waters of those sacred lakes and from this intercourse the people emerged. That is why there is so much power in that piace; it is the source.

"Either way you would have it, the people settled along the river valley that ran by the mountain. The tribe grew and prospered, for on one side they were guarded by their sacred mountain and on the other by the burning, white desert. The valley was fertile, the fruits of the trees were sweet, and corn and beans and squash grew abundantly. The people lived in peace and harmony with the earth and her gods.

"But not all of the gods were loving gods. The simple dance feasts and the offerings of animals and vegetables grew monotonous to those gods who took their strength from fear, famine, pestilence and death. They demanded human sacrifice! The wise priests of the people consulted for seven days and seven nights, then they returned to the gods, and speaking as respectfully as they could, refused to sacrifice their brethren. The gods grew angry, and to punish the people they stole away the sun. They took the life-giving golden deer and spirited him away to the south and there they entombed him in the pit of a dark volcano. Unending night fell upon Aztlán. Without the sun the plants wilted and died, and the earth shriveled with cold. Death stole from home to home. Fear ruled. The people dressed in mourning clothes and grieved the end of the world."

Crispín paused, and Clemente felt in his sigh the ending of an age.

Outside the fury of the storm reached its height; the wind made the small house shudder; the tempest seemed to rock the earth herself. And Clemente felt as the people of Aztlán must have felt when eternal darkness fell upon them.

Crispín continued.

"——Then there appeared in the dark void another god. He came in the form of a fiery serpent and the light he cast was so bright it lit up all of Aztlán. The people fell on their knees and asked deliverance of the bright plumed god whose tail shone so brightly it turned the night to day. And he answered their prayers by walking among them and renewing the life of their fields, and ministering to those who were sick, and conversing with the wise priests. And he spoke to the people of Aztlán and made a covenant with them. He told them to leave their home in Aztlán, promising that someday they would return, but now they were to travel south. There they were to settle and build their new civilization. He promised them the sun god would be freed because the old gods would cast themselves into the pit of the volcano, and their sacrifice would give him the power to rise again. So an old age would end, and a new one would begin under the protection of the long serpent who spoke wisely and whose plumes were made of fire.

"The people obeyed, and it is said he lighted up the skies as they marched south. And it is said that all these things the god promised were delivered, and the people flourished and built a civilization without equal. And always their first thanks were to the serpent god and to the sun. Later, old gods were resurrected, and again they quarreled, this time with enough force to banish the wise god who had walked among the people. He streaked to the east into the arms of his brother sun, but he promised to return——"

For a long time they sat in silence, sipping hot coffee and smoking. They knew the story of the return.

"——And the singing rocks? " Clemente asked, "Where do they come from? Are they part of the legend? "

"Yes," Crispín nodded. "The god's tail was made of fire, but when he walked on earth the fire cooled and turned into rocks with strange and magical powers. The rocks contained the melody of the universe within them, and they could speak and cure people. They were part of the covenant, and the history of the people was inscribed in them for future generations to know, but when the plumed god was cast out the rocks lost their power of good, and they became las piedras malas del mundo, stones with evil properties which evil men extract to do their bidding——"

"La piedra mala," Clemente whispered. "The old witch by the water, she has one."

"Perhaps," Crispín nodded, "anyway, no harm can come to one who keeps a piedra mala. They live forever——"

"Forever——" Clemente shuddered. He remembered looking into the old woman's withered face. It was the face of eternity.

"How does one know if the rock is a piedra mala? " He asked.

Crispín rose and went to an old trunk he kept at the foot of his bed. He took out a small pouch and showed it to Clemente. It contained a handful of needles and pins. "They are made of silver," he said, "the black rock devours them. Only then can you speak with it——"

Clemente remembered the searing shock he had received from la piedra mala. It was because he had not been prepared. Now he could return and draw the secrets from the black stone, now he knew how to make it answer. He threw off the blanket with which Crispín had covered him and stood up. He felt dizzy, debilitated from months of drinking, weak from the cold, and hungry from so many months of not caring whether he lived or not.

"You are too weak to move yet," Crispín said.

"No, no," Clemente shook his head, "I must start now, there is no time to waste. I see now that the journey of the people was out

125

of Aztlán. They never forgot the heartland, it called them back, and they returned, a new people, under a new guise, they now bore new gods upon their backs, they now sought gold—— But that is not why they returned! " He laughed and shivered with fever, "It was because the throbbing of the heart called them back! Hundreds of years passed and they never forgot the home-land! They returned to complete the cycle. Now I must move in search of that source of strength——"

Crispín also stood. "I will go with you," he said.

"It will be a long journey," Clemente said.

Crispín simply smiled. "All of life is a journey, and each day we begin it anew. The storm is quiet now; it is a good time to start."

"Gracias," Clemente thanked his friend and placed his hands on the old man's shoulders. He knew they were bound to follow the whispers of the four winds, wherever they led.

"I want to visit the old woman," Clemente said, "if only to rid myself of the fear of the past. If she truly possesses a magic rock that has been handed down through the ages, then going there is like going to the very beginning——"

"True," Crispín agreed. He picked up his blue guitar and slung it over his shoulder. It was his only prized possession, everything else in the hut was but the rubble accumulated in life and of no consequence. But his guitar contained the poems yet to be sung, the simple truths to be discovered, and the melody that would make time stand still.

Crispín felt Clemente's passion. He swung his serape over his shoulders and called out, "I am ready! "

They walked into the cold, early morning. It was still dark, but the raging wind had died. The stars sparkled in the clear, dark ocean of the universe. The snow and frozen earth crunched be-neath their feet as they worked their way towards the dark corner of their barrio. Somewhere a dog barked, braving the cold to cry a warning. Otherwise around them, the still and awful presence of the universe moaned indifferently at the two intruders that dis-turbed the night.

Crispín seemed to know his way through the jungle of brush. They arrived at a clearing and he nodded to Clemente.

"There is a light," Clemente whispered.

"She never sleeps," Crispín answered, "she cannot sleep," he added, "she must keep eternal vigilance over the magic rock——"

Clemente shivered. He remembered the first visit to the hut and the terrible nightmare it had become. He gathered his courage and started forward, but Crispín stopped him. "You will need these——" He opened the pouch and gave the handful of pins and needles to Clemente. "When she tells you to place your hand on the rock, first put these on it."

They walked to the door and knocked. There was a long silence, then a hoarse voice called, "¿Quién es, diablo o hombre? "

" ¡Hombres de carne y hueso! " Crispín shouted, "A blind old man and a fool who would speak to your piedra mala! "

The voice cackled with laughter, and the door opened to allow them to enter. A cat bristled and hissed from a dark corner of the dimly lighted room. The stench from the pot brewing at the stove permeated the small room. "Entren, entren," the old woman beckoned them in with bony fingers. They entered and the door slammed shut behind them. She laughed and greeted them.

"Ay, Crispín, I see you still carry that battered, old guitar with you," she sneered.

"It is an old and faithful companion," Crispín smiled, "when it is by my side all the black magic of the world cannot touch me."

Clemente understood that they knew each other, and that they tested each other with their greetings.

"Bah! " She scoffed, "I told you many years ago that those enchanting melodies you seek would be yours, if only——"

"——If only I sold my soul to the powers of your rock," Crispín interjected and nodded at the lump on the table. La piedra mala seemed to breathe beneath its cover.

"True! True! " The old woman clapped her hands and hissed with laughter. "We know of your powers, Crispín, blinded though you are you can see beyond most men! We would welcome you in the service of La Piedra! "

Crispín shook his head. "Tell la piedra mala that I will find my way in my darkness without selling my soul——"

"Fool! " The old witch screeched in anger, "You blind, old fool! You know the power in the rock! You know the vision in its web and still you do not bow to it! You will die seeking the melody that will make you the brother of time and death, while I will never die! " she boasted and her rheumy eyes flashed with yellow fire. "I will never die! I measure my time in centuries! "

Crispín shrugged. "I do not judge the wisdom of living forever—— your flesh withers and people shiver when you pass.
Anyway, I did not come to make idle conversation. Tonight it is
my friend who seeks to know the power in the rock . . ."

"Bah! " she spit in disappointment. "I have no use for this
weakling. He touched the rock and whimpered like a dog! " She
turned to Clemente and laughed. "Look at him! He is trembling
with fever. He is near death . . ."

"It was an unfair encounter! " Crispín said sternly. "You did
not instruct him properly! "

The old bruja cringed. She turned to Clemente and looked at him,
then she shook her head. "Even if I consented," she said, "the vision
in the rock would burn him dry. You have brought me a dying man
. . ."

"No! " Clemente insisted. "I am not yet dead, and I will not die
until I have touched the heart of my land . . . the soul of my
people! " His body trembled and ached with fever, but he would
not be denied.

"Did he bring the gift? " the old woman muttered. Clemente
opened his bleeding hand and showed her the silver pins. "Very
well," she relented, "but if he dies tonight then it is you who will
have to drag his body to the water——"

"I am going with him," Crispín said.

"No! " the old witch protested, "Don't be a fool! I have
already told you, his chances are not good! Look at him, he's
near death! And if he finds the caverns at the top of those
mountains he'll drown you in their water! He'll drown both of
you! "

"I will walk with him," Crispín whispered, and the old woman
backed away, muttering that she would bury them both.

She turned to Clemente and made him sit facing the rock, and
she instructed him carefully. First he was to place the silver pins
and needles on the rock, and when he did it seemed to writhe with
life. The pins disappeared slowly. Clemente felt his stomach heave
and he turned to find Crispín, but the old woman hissed a sharp
command: "Look at the rock! It is death to look anywhere
except at the rock! Look only at the fire in the rock . . . You will
enter the rock . . . You will find the door in a grain of sand . . .

128

you will find the door to the mountain . . . you will find the seven wombs of the earth . . ." She began to chant and the room began to spin slowly around the rock.

The journey began. Clemente was aware of the preparations. He saw Crispín get ready and he repeated the motions of the old man. The shining rock became a door which they could enter. At the entrance the old woman greeted them. She gave Clemente a bitter potion to drink; it fell like bile into his empty stomach and a numbing sensation spread throughout his body, quieting the swirling vertigo. She pointed and again he looked at the rock and this time a melody drew him into the river in which the rock tumbled.

The water was the color of dark earth and blood. People tumbled like driftwood in a spring-flooded river. Each ghost clutched at him and cried for help.

Deliver us, Clemente Chávez! they cried, and Clemente drew back in horror.

Strike down the snakes of steel that bind our soul, the people cried. Deliver us from this oppression! Strike down injustice!

And Clemente cried in agony because he didn't know how to help the fish-people which the swirling river carried past him. My God, my God, he groaned, give me the strength, give me the power to help my people!

He turned to Crispín for help, and the blind poet touched him and lifted him out of the dark shades toward the south. In the land of the south they walked among the ruins where ancient gods once lived and died, and on the facades of crumbling temples they read the sacred signs.

Long ago, the scripture whispered, the people came.

Everywhere the wind moaned with the name of their homeland. They sat with old caciques who told the stories of the past, and always the four directions were pointed out, and in the center stood Aztlán.

They moved north, and there Aztlán was a woman fringed with snow and ice; they moved west, and there she was a mermaid singing by the sea; and always, beneath the form in the vision they heard the soft throbbing of her heart. They walked to the land where the sun rises, and there by the side of the sea where the morning star and the sun played upon the waves before day entered, they found new signs, and the signs pointed them back to

129

the center, back to Aztlán.

Where? Clemente cried in pain, Oh where is the source of my river!

There, the wind answered, there where the seven springs form the sacred lake! There by the desert of the white herons!

And they traveled on, following new signs, listening to the secrets of whispered stories, moving towards the center. The sun burned them to the bone, the fever dried Clemente's soul so he could not speak, and the mountain trails cut his feet until they bled, and still he moved forward, whispering the name Aztlán.

High on a mountain they met the keeper of the magic rock, and when Clemente begged for a sign she pointed at the rock. Two forms rose from the lump of the earth. One was a man clad in shining scales and the other was a woman dressed in feathers. They mated, twisting together like snakes, forming the tree which Clemente climbed, and from which he soared like a giant bird. He saw the burning desert of the legend! He saw the sacred mountain to the east! And he caught a glimpse of the sacred lake!

I know this place, he whispered.

It is the center, Crispín answered, and Clemente understood that he had begun his journey here. The river lapped at his feet, the waters sang a song of life. Deserted mud-castles crumbled in the silence of the desert. Beneath him he felt the heart of his earth and he knew that he was near.

Behind him he heard Crispín's blessing, and then he entered the desert alone, and he re-entered it again and again until he found the door in the grain of sand, and he found the path to the mountain's lake. With a last effort he pushed himself up the glowing mountain, up the steep palisades anchored to the earth by dark pines, past the last web of rock that blocked the entrance to the holy place. Torn and bleeding and barely alive he found himself on a moonlit meadow at the edge of the sacred lake. The river of the manswarm rushed past him, gushing up from the depths of the lake, thundering by him to the beat of the pumping heart. And again the people called as they rushed by him.

¡Injusticia! the long lines of men bound in chains of steel called to him.

¡Miseria! frail, skeletal women cried as they gathered hungry children to their withered breasts.

¡Pobresa! the masses echoed, and the torrent was so strong it
lifted him up and tossed him into the raging waters. The river at its
source sang with the same message of the wind; it whispered that
he was Aztlán, and when he understood that, he could reach out
and touch his people. Wounds opened in his hands. He held his
breath and thrust deeper into the river of the manswarm, mixing
his blood with theirs, swimming against the groaning waters, diving
deeper into the lake until he saw the seven springs. There at the
core lay the dark, pounding heart. He had come to the source of
life and time and history. He reached out and grasped with
bleeding hands the living heart of the earth.

Time stood still, and in that enduring moment he felt the
rhythm of the heart of Aztlán beat to the measure of his own
heart. Dreams and visions became reality, and reality was but the
thin substance of myth and legends. A joyful power coursed from
the dark womb-heart of the earth into his soul and he cried out I
AM AZTLÁN!

My heart is the heart of the earth!
I am the earth and I am the blue sky!
I am the water and I am the wind!
I walk in legends told today, and turn and recreate the past . . .
I pause and give the future time to grow.
I am the image, and I am the living man!
I am the dream, I am the waking . . .

Aztlán, Aztlán, the waters sang, and he raised his torn and
bleeding hands and smeared the blood of the dark earth on his
face. He had come to the source and he understood the bond they
shared, he was one of them. There was no special grace or
deliverance in the pain he felt, only a thin bond of comradeship to
the masses that floated down the river of time into a new beginning. Knowing this he accepted death and let the water take its
course.

Deliverance, the river moaned, and cutting a new channel into
the future it tossed him upon a mossy bank.

Clemente gasped for breath and felt the searing pain of reality
returning. Far down the mountain, in the swirling mist of dawn,
he heard the music of the blue guitar. Crispín was coming to help;
he would not let him die. The old man was challenging the
mountain once again. He would light a fire to warm him, and

131

when the sun rose he would offer the sacred corn meal to the sun and the wind and the four directions. Then he would mix the blue corn meal with the holy water of the lake and make the simple food of life.

An owl called and Clemente smiled. Blood and dried earth encrusted his body, but he felt very much alive. The images he had seen were already receding, but it didn't matter, he had touched the heart of his sacred earth and that would be with him forever. He heard a lustful shout roll down the mountain, and when the sound returned he recognized his voice in el grito that tore away the darkness and raised the sun.

CHAPTER FOURTEEN

And so Clemente returned to the barrio, barely alive, raving about the mountain he had climbed and the visions he had seen. Fever racked his body as he lay in bed and for weeks he alternated between fitful sleep and wild explosions when he repeated his journey. Bits of the story drifted out into the cold barrio streets and wherever the men gathered to talk they talked about Clemente.

"He was gone a long time," one said, "no one knows where, but he came back crazy . . . His hair has grown long, like a wild man. He is dying, they say . . ."

"Some say he sold his soul to la piedra . . ."

"They say he talks about a mountain, and a river of people . . . can you imagine that, compadre, a river of people? Some say they were both nearly dead when they found them . . . It was an old Indian who found them in the mountains, a man who had once killed a deer and found a sliver of bone as long as your finger in its heart. Ay, what a contradiction to encounter in life, eh, a piece of bone in a deer's heart . . . I would not look at that for all the money in the world. It would drive me crazy . . ."

"And the old Indian brought them down? "

"Bah! Rumors! " Lalo spit. "They got drunk and now they're dying of malnutrition! They nearly froze to death in an alley, not on a magic mountain! "

"Crispín doesn't drink," old Manuel corrected him. "No, there's something more than that here . . . I feel sorry for him; he lives in a pesadilla he cannot break. I cannot tell when he's making sense or raving about the wild nightmares he suffers, but his eyes burn with power——"

"Insanity! " Lalo laughed, but the men did not join him.

"No," Manuel shook his head, "no, it's not insanity . . . or if it is, it's the same insanity that drove the prophets to the desert . . ."

Three men from south Barelas joined the group for a moment; they asked about Clemente and when told that he was resting they moved on.

"——Anyway, it's bullets we need, not prophets! " Lalo said when they were gone. "The only thing those bastards understand is power! " And he pointed towards the shops.

Inside the house Clemente's family cared for him and for Crispín.

"He will not rest," Adelita moaned, "he keeps wanting to get up. He says he has found a way to bind the people together. Santo Niño de Atocha, he is so weak he cannot move, and still he wants to rise . . ."

"He keeps repeating he has touched the heart of the earth, that he has seen the truth," Juanita added.

"The truth? " Adelita swallowed bitterly. She pushed back the hair on her forehead and shook her head. "Is it truth that makes a man mad like an animal? Yes, it was a wounded and dying animal they found, delirious with fever, shouting wild stories . . . And poor Crispín. Did he also look upon that truth? " She shook her head sadly and looked at the old man who slept by the wall heater, letting the heat drive the weariness out of his cold bones. "Why don't they forget these truths that drive them to the edge of death, or insanity——"

"He isn't insane! " Juanita spoke up. Her harshness startled them, and she muttered, "it's just that he has suffered much——"

"No, he's not insane," Adelita agreed, and she gently touched her husband's cheek. "But I don't know what he was doing on that cursed mountain he talks about. Your father is not a man of the mountains, he is a man of the llano, a man of the flat country where the hills are smooth and gentle. The sweet piñon and the bushy juniper are his trees, not the towering pine; and the nopal and palmilla are his flowers, not the lupine of the mountain meadows. The waters he knows flow from gentle springs, not from roaring, mountain streams. A man can get lost in the deep canyons of the mountains, but on the llano your father was never lost.

There is always the bright sun to guide the man, always the wind blowing in one direction——" Tears filled her eyes. "Why did he go? " She asked. "What did he expect to find? "

"I don't know," Juanita said after a long silence, "but I am glad he went, I don't know why, but I am. It would have been easier for him to give up as he grew older, he has three women to cater to his needs, and growing sons to bring him grandchildren. It would have been easier to dream in the sun on the porch, instead he followed his dreams wherever they led, and I am glad he went——"

Adelita nodded. What her daughter said was true. "Ah, those dreams," she murmured, "it seems that's all there is to life, a seeking after dreams ..." She shrugged and walked into the kitchen. She felt bitter, because she felt her husband's pain and anguish, but she put aside her rancor to care for him. Her love for him had begun long ago and they had been through too much together for her to turn away. And so she nursed him back to life. Long into the nights she sat by him and placed cold packs on his emaciated body, until she broke his fever. Day after day she coaxed food into him until he regained enough strength to sit and eat. She listened to his story until it was complete, and only she understood what he had been through. And when he could rise and walk she helped him dress and understood why he had to continue his search.

"I will go to the priest," he whispered, "he will know what to do. Then I will go to the men, they are meeting tonight ..."

"I should have cut your hair, and shaved you," she said simply, "you look like a wild man——"

He held her gently and looked into her eyes. "No, it is better this way ... Manuel has said the men think I'm crazy, well then, perhaps I am ... if so, I will act like one."

She touched the black beard on his face. Once his face had been brown and healthy, now it was pale and drawn, and his eyes that used to bring her joy now burned through her and made her tremble. "You are still very weak, and it's so cold outside ..."

He held his fingers to her lips. "I must go," he said, "help me by letting me do what I must do." Then he held her for a moment and whispered, "Oh, Adela, there will be a time when we can live in peace again ... but we must make that time now." He kissed her and quickly walked away.

He followed the alley towards the church, and by the time he reached the towering edifice he was trembling and sweating from exhaustion. He approached the church tremulously. He had no need for the priest, but while he lay recovering from his illness he had resolved to seek the priest's counsel. The vision of the movement of the people was clear to Clemente, and it was just as clear that everyone had to be included in the rushing time wherein their destiny was forged. Yes, he thought as he neared the shadows of the church, the priest has seen the oppression the people suffer, and he has the ability to help. He is an educated man; he understands the law and how it should protect the people. He can advise us of our rights. With his help the barrio would stand united and soon the pressure they could exert would spread throughout the city ... The dams that kept the people in check would be broken and the river would flow with the power he had seen in his dreams.

Clemente smiled. He was glad he had resolved to come. He felt very weak, but the sense of reaching out and gathering the forces needed for the struggle buoyed his spirit. With luck the priest would even attend the meeting tonight, and the winter of waiting would be over.

In the dark the church towered over him. It stood like a fortress in the middle of the barrio. Clemente hesitated at the door of the rectory. He knew that Lalo's group did not trust Father Cayo, and their contempt for the old priest was such that they spit in front of the church instead of making the sign of the cross and asking God's help. He knew that the bad feelings were caused when the first organizers of the strike came to the priest for help and he turned them down. He had not only refused them support but he had castigated them and called them troublemakers. He had warned them to let things remain as they were because the strike would only bring turmoil to the quiet barrio and suffering to the people. He had even threatened them with excommunication. When the first group of strikers were fired and the welfare line grew, he preached triumphantly from his pulpit, saying that he had warned the handful of communist organizers to leave things as they were. He blamed the troubles of the people on these radicals, and he warned the people of the barrio to stay away from them.

Clemente had heard the story more then once, and he understood the division that it had caused among the workers from the barrio. It had been difficult to protest for change after that, and much more difficult to organize. But Clemente granted the priest the benefit of the doubt. Perhaps the man had not been approached in the right manner, and perhaps he lived so isolated in the church that he did not see the plight of the people around him. Maybe the padrecito in his old age had forgotten that at one time priests were the leaders of revolutions for the rights of men, and that it was Hidalgo, a poor village priest, who had earned a place in the heart of the people because he dared to cry out against injustice. El Grito de Dolores, Clemente thought, it was a part of the history told in the cuentos of Crispín. But the priests of the people had forgotten and grown fat and lazy in the comfort of their parishes. Perhaps it was not entirely their fault they lost their huevos, too many French and Irish priests had been brought in to serve a people they didn't understand, and in most cases they had kept the people down.

Clemente sighed and knocked on the door of the church. He would not pre-judge the man. He simply wanted to talk to him and present his ideas and seek his advice. The housekeeper answered the door.

"What do you want? " She asked gruffly.

"I want to see the padre," Clemente answered.

"Eh? " she said and cupped her hand at her ear. She was a stooped, old woman, offsetting her decline in years with makeup and jewelry, but actually hard of hearing. "What is it you want? " she repeated.

"I want to see the priest! " Clemente shouted.

"Do you have an appointment? " she asked and looked him over carefully.

"No, no," Clemente shook his head, "I have no appointment, I simply want to see the priest——"

"Father Cayo is eating supper . . . He cannot be disturbed! " She shook her head. She started to close the door but Clemente pushed it open and stepped inside.

"I have to see the priest! " he insisted. "It's a matter of life and death."

His aggressive manner startled her. "Eh? " she cried, "Whose death? Who's dying? You can't come in like this! It's unheard of——"

"Call the padre! " Clemente insisted. "He will understand."

"Humph! " the old housekeeper rubbed her hands and backed away, "Wait there." She pointed at a bench then disappeared into a dark doorway.

Clemente waited for a long time in the cold, lifeless parlor, but at length Father Cayo appeared. He walked in ceremoniously, took a chair across the room from Clemente and did not speak until he had lighted a cigar.

"What do you want? " he asked coldly.

"I am Clemente Chávez," Clemente answered respectfully. "I came because——"

"You came to confess! " the priest interrupted him.

Clemente felt confused. The priest must have mistaken him for someone else. "No, padre," he shook his head, "I did not come to confess——"

"But you are in need of confession and repentance! " the priest shouted across the room. "You need to have your sins absolved because you have consorted with the evil woman! The fortune teller! "

"No, padre," Clemente repeated, "there is nothing to confess." The priest's outburst surprised him.

"I know her ways! " Father Cayo charged. "She deals in black magic, brujerías! She reads the Black Book! " he shouted and then crossed himself and added, "Holy be the name of God . . . It is known you sold your soul to the devil! " he finished and pointed an accusing finger.

"No! " Clemente answered, "I did not! Those are evil rumors——"

"Then why did you go to that evil place? Do you deny that you visited her? "

"I don't deny it, padre," Clemente answered calmly. "I went because I heard there was power in the old woman's rock . . . I sought understanding——"

"If it was understanding you sought why didn't you come to the house of God! " the priest interrupted again. "God is all the knowledge you need! You should have come on your knees to God! "

138

"I am here now," Clemente said simply. "I have come to ask your help."

Father Cayo gasped. "Beware, Clemente Chávez," he exclaimed, "don't play word games with me! If it's an argument you want you are no match for me! " He coughed and threw his cigar aside. "The truth of the matter is that you went to that evil woman, and everyone is whispering that you claim to have acquired strange powers! " He made his accusation and looked closely at Clemente. It was hard to imagine that the people were gathering around this sick, wild-looking man.

"I don't claim any powers," Clemente answered, "the people believe what they want. I have simply spoken about my journey and about the dreams I have in which my people call to me for help . . . That's all I want to do, to help them. That's why I came here tonight——"

"Why? " the priest chuckled, "Was I in your vision? "

"Yes, yes! " Clemented nodded enthusiastically. "Everyone shares in it! From the holy heart of the earth a river of people gushes forth and——"

"Enough! " the priest cried out. "I cannot hear such blasphemy! María! María! " he choked and called for the housekeeper, "more wine, María, please . . ." He pointed at his glass and massaged his throat. The arthritic old woman nervously poured the drink which he swallowed quickly to stop his trembling. "Good," he said when he could breathe again, "now go away! " He motioned her away and loosened his collar. He looked at Clemente who stood looking at the books that lined one wall of the study. I am a fool, the priest smiled to himself, to let this simple, wild man upset me like this. He composed himself and spoke to Clemente.

"So, the men are gathering around you and calling you their leader, Chávez . . . What is it you expect of me? "

"Yes, the men want me to speak to them tonight . . . they wait for a message . . . but I am not a leader," Clemente said. "I am a weak man, and a leader must be a strong, spiritual person . . . like you." He looked at the priest.

Father Cayo shivered. The man's words unnerved him and caused him to reflect. ". . . Yes, I have been a leader for many years," he nodded. "I have cared for my people . . . I baptize their

139

children, I hear their confessions and give them absolution for their sins, I marry them . . . and when they die I pray the Mass of the Dead for them. I have followed over a thousand processions from my church to the campo santo to pray at their gravesides . . . to sanctify the earth . . . And I give courage to the living so that they may go on living," he sighed and looked at Clemente. "What more do you expect of me . . ."

"That would be more than enough in times of peace and order," Clemente agreed, "but we're at war! Yes, the struggle to throw off the chains of oppression is a war, and to do battle the people need a strong man who will lead them! The enemy understands this! They have drawn the battle line and mapped out their strategy, and that is why they can cut us down at every move! The workers need someone who understands the complexity of that struggle . . . a general——" He finished in a whisper. He was pale and weak from his long stay in bed. He had pushed himself too soon to carry out his mission; the fever crept in again and he trembled with cold shivers. He felt his body wet with sweat.

"A general indeed! " the priest laughed. "No, there is nothing I can do——"

"You can at least speak out! " Clemente insisted.

"I do speak out! " the priest hissed back. "I lecture the people every Sunday at mass! "

"Oh God," Clemente groaned, "I don't mean sermons, padre! You have to speak out against the tyranny of the shops! We don't need the gospels, we need the fiery men who wrote them! " He slammed his fist on the table.

"Don't be sacreligious Chávez! " Father Cayo shouted back. "What you say are grounds for excommunication! "

Clemente laughed bitterly. His patience with the priest was exhausted and his strength gone. He shook his head slowly and his feverish stare cut through the priest.

"Padre," he said, "I don't give a damn about your excommunication, and as far as I know most of the men don't either! The simple truth is that the workers need a strong leader. Without a leader to organize the struggle our efforts are too spread out and weak . . . Some want to burn down the shops, others want to follow the court suit and wait, still others want to give in and return ... But a strong man could unite the workers, and right now you are in the position to bring about this unity! If you spoke against the injustice we suffer the entire barrio would unite behind you! With that kind of power we could close down the shops! The bosses would have to negotiate! "

Clemente's eyes burned with the fervor he felt.

"——And don't you see," he continued, "this victory would create ripples across the land! It would be the start of a new movement; a struggle for justice that would sweep across the land would be born right here! Everywhere, men and women would unite and raise the cry that human decency and justice should prevail! "

Father Cayo groaned. "You preach revolution, Chávez, but you don't understand that the church can't join it! The Church has discussed movements like yours many times, and the orders are very explicit on this matter ... We are not to get mixed up in these political struggles! It's that simple. The work of the Church is to care for the souls of men; that is its primary responsibility, and from that goal it will never waver! These complaints of the workers are fired by the whims of radicals; and the political affiliations of the masses change from one day to the next ... Tomorrow another cause arises and the pendulum swings the other way. The workers are swayed by their emotions, and they sell themselves to the cause that offers them more money. History teaches us that, Chávez ... but you probably can't even read," he added.

"It is true I am an uneducated man, padre, that is why I came to you," Clemente agreed.

"But where would the stability of the church be if it joined every movement that reared its head from the gutters of the barrio! " the priest roared back. "The church cannot commit itself to these temporal movements. Its primary commitment is to save your soul, the souls that belong to God ... The Church has found a perfect cause, Chávez, a cause that never changes! That is why it has survived for centuries! Men come and go, and their political philosophies follow them to the grave, and the revolutions they create in turn engender counter-revolutions, and the cycle repeats itself forever ... but the Church remains! It exists for all time ... because it has found the perfect cause," he whispered.

Father Cayo sat back and smiled. "So, if we have our own

141

cause, why should we jeopardize our existence to join yours? " he asked.

"The people——" Clemente pleaded.

"Bah! Do you think the poor people of the barrio pay for the upkeep of the Church? No! Wealth flows from wealth! And sources of wealth need stability to exist! And the Church provides stability! We teach the poor how to bear their burden; they are promised the kingdom of heaven, which is far more important than the little gains your strike would make . . ."

He paused and saw the consternation spread across Clemente's face. He took time to fix a cigar and light it. The thin smoke spread out in plumes, swirling tongues licking at the stale air of the study.

"Don't think it so strange, Chávez, it's true . . . The Church is a goliath, as big and as powerful as the rest. And there is security and order in its size. If there is one thing history has taught us, it is that there is peace only in stability. No one profits from times of revolution, Chávez, no one, not even the poor. You look surprised, but it is true. Look at history, it is stability and order that have improved the lot of the masses, not revolution. When there is change everyone suffers. The winds of change are like a fire, kindled by the basest emotions of man, and driving a plague before them that destroys everything in its path! When old empires topple the consequences are far-reaching, and he who hurries their destruction by revolution must be responsible for the famine and suffering that follows—— And worse, much worse! " He shook his finger to make his point. "In the end, another empire, another structure rises from the ashes of all that misery and destruction, and we can never be sure that its rule will be more just or its methods more humane than those of its prede- cessor. Think on that, Chávez, think on it, then let things remain as they are——"

Clemente shrugged. "I cannot let things remain as they are, because then I would not be free. If I cease to act because I fear the future, then I create a worse enslavement for myself. That much I know. While my people are not free, I am not free. If the freedom and justice I seek loose destruction upon the earth, then I accept that responsibility, but it seems to me that the real respon- sibility must be borne by those who keep me from my freedom. I

142

must act! And I ask you, will you lend your help or not! "

"Ay, Chávez," the priest groaned, "nothing I have said makes sense to you . . . You don't understand the intricate rules that keep the giants in balance . . . the government, the banks, the military, the church . . . all must respect each other, because they know to turn on each other would bring destruction to all. They protect each other out of necessity, and they realize that the man who finds the key to destroy one of them can destroy them all . . . My hands are tied."

Clemente sat silent for a long time. He knew the enemy was big and complex and that was why he had come to the priest for help, but now he understood that there were many monsters and that if perchance a man cut down one frightful head another reared up in its place. The struggle before him was monumental, but perhaps the priest had inadvertently given him a clue. He had suggested that there was a key, a weak spot perhaps, a soft spot in the belly of these monstrous serpents.

"Then I will find that key," he answered the priest, "I will find that sword that will cut through and make blood run from hearts of steel! The soul of the people will be liberated from the steel that traps it——"

Father Cayo trembled. He could not control the wave of help-lessness that drained his body. He looked at Clemente's burning eyes and at the explosive tension coiled in every muscle, and he shivered. He could almost hear Clemente's heart beating, and the sound frightened him. He found himself saying, "——I fear you, Chávez, I fear your pure and simple faith. You don't understand the powers you challenge, and still you are willing to move ahead. It is possible—by the farthest stretch of the imagination—it is possible that you could bring the whole thing toppling down on us, destroying everything. You are insane because you are willing to take that consequence, and if it ever comes to be, the saddest part is that you will never realize what you have let loose upon the world through your insanity. If your revolution comes it will take you down also, and you will be destroyed by the terrible forces you unleash——"

"Then let us do it together! " Clemente pleaded. "You under-stand those forces, and your wise guidance can assure us that the people will not suffer because of what you do! I did not come to ask anything for myself, no, I came to plead the case of those men out there whose families are going hungry! Join us! Be their leader! They will listen to you——" He could say no more. His throat felt parched. The fever was returning and with it came the images of the surging river. He moaned because he knew he had failed to convince the priest, and so he would return to the men with empty hands.

"I cannot! " the priest said adamantly. They stared at each other in the empty silence.

"Then I will do it alone," Clemente whispered. "I will find a way . . . that is my task . . ."

"Oh my God," the priest moaned, "the people whisper about you and call you a deliverer. Why did you have to come to this miserable barrio! " he shouted and fell back into his chair and laughed hysterically. "Why do the multitudes follow madmen? Why? " he cursed and bowed his head.

Outside the north wind blew against the church and rattled its windows like the wind of the desert rattles over dry bones. Clemente rose to leave. He felt very tired and old. He had been so sure that the priest would speak out against the injustices the workers suffered; instead he had encountered adamant opposition. A sense of futility drained his body of its strength. The fever had built up and Clemente knew it would soon drag him down, but before it did he vowed to meet with the men and bring them some sense of hope. He paused at the door and turned.

"The men are meeting tonight, padre . . . come with me. They will listen to you . . ."

"Go away, Chávez," the priest sighed, "leave me alone . . ."

Clemente walked out into the cold night. He pulled his coat around him and walked slowly to Crispín's hut where the strikers were meeting. As he walked he planned his next move. He would go to el Super. The man was a businessman, and he would understand the negotiation procedures and how to deal with the injunctions of the court. He made his living from the people, so surely he would show his gratitude by helping them. Clemente had vowed to find the right person who could lead the strike, and he would not be deterred by his failure to enlist the priest. And so struggling against the fever and thinking of the plan he would follow, he entered the roomful of men. The men turned to greet him. It was the first time they had seen him since his sickness, but each one had heard bits of the story of Clemente's journey and all were strangely drawn to this man from Guadalaupe. They were eager to hear from him, but in deference to Lalo they turned their attention back to him.

"Goddammit! " Lalo shouted and slammed his fist on the wooden table to regain their attention, "We can't go on without work! There's nothing left! The whole city's closed against us. I ask for a job and the minute they hear my name they tell me to leave! Why is it the court injunction is against us and not against the businessmen who practice blacklisting! "

"And against the scabs! " a man shouted.

"The vise is shutting us out of everything," Lalo continued, "the men we started with have given up and moved away . . . I don't blame them; I ran out of money a long time ago. The welfare check pays for the rent, and that's it! My children throw up that rotten welfare food, and they grow sick. Now my woman wants to work, to clean houses for the gringos at the Country Club—— Hell no! I say no! What will become of our families! " He was a hard, powerful man, but his voice quivered with emotion. He spit with contempt to recover his composure. "I will not allow that! "

"We're all in the same boat! " Wild Héctor cried. The two had been together since the first efforts to organize the workers. The men knew that the two went armed.

"That's what the welfare people want," Tranquilino gritted his teeth, "to have us on welfare and to have our women working. Then they can point to our broken families and say the mexicano is a lazy, no good son-of-a-bitch! Well, I too am tired of that. I tried to speak with men of reason, I kept saying let's go slow, but it's no use. They don't listen. I'm sick and tired of it! " He spit in disgust.

"Then you say we go with Lalo? " Someone asked.

"Yes! " Tranquilino cried back angrily, defeated. He had seen his family go cold and grow sick that winter for want of food, and he had felt the threat of the blacklist which kept him from a job. Nothing mattered anymore.

" ¡Andale! " Wild-eyed Héctor shouted, "Now you're talking! We wanted work and they gave us rancid butter and corn meal

145

dirty with bugs! Everywhere we went looking for a job they called us trouble-makers and turned us away, until they had broken our backs and cut off our huevos, and most of our brothers gave up and left, or learned to survive by sucking! We cannot survive the winter. Those jobs and rights we ask for are rightfully ours! Our sweat and blood built the Santa Fe and the Southern Pacific and all the rest! Our souls are trapped in that steel, and the only way to free them is with this! " He brandished his pistol from beneath his jacket.

"Ten paciencia," old Manuel tried to cool him down, "violence will get us nowhere——"

"We're tired of patience! " Lalo barked like a dog of war, "Patience hasn't gotten us anywhere either! Strikebreakers are being hired every day, and I'm supposed to be patient! Our women have to work to support our families, and I'm supposed to be patient! The hell with it! It's time we met force with force, an eye for an eye! That's the only rule those sons-of-bitches understand! "

The small group that followed Lalo and Héctor agreed, the rest of the men were silent.

"——Maybe it's the only rule they understand," Manuel agreed, "but they are too big and powerful, and the law is on their side. It would be like walking into a lion's den unarmed, we would lose. Most of the suffering would be ours."

"Then the only other alternative is to wear them down, to hit at their profits, until they sit down at the table to bargain——" It was Primo who spoke.

"Yes," Manuel answered, "the fly armed with only a buzzing sound got in the lion's ear and molested him until the powerful and savage lion scratched his brains out in irritation. So we must be like the fly, constantly buzzing our truths in this giant's ear, chingandolo, chingandolo, chingandolo——"

The men laughed. But it was an uneasy laughter, because they knew how long it would take to wear down that monstrosity they fought. If it was the only way to proceed, then it was a long and weary road.

"Why do we continue," one of them whispered out of the dim light, "perhaps it would be best to forget the struggle, to give in——"

146

"No! " Lalo shouted. "It's a just struggle! We can't give that up! Don't you see, it's not just us, it's all of the people across the land——" He paused and looked at them and felt his words fell on many deaf ears. Suddenly the exhaustion of the struggle overwhelmed him. He took the bottle of Tokay wine his friend handed him and swallowed hard to wash away the bitterness. "Clemente," he handed the bottle to Clemente. "What do you think? "

Clemente held the bottle for a long time, gazing at the dark contents, and then he passed the bottle so that each man sipped the sweet, warm wine. They did not drink to get drunk, but to share in the communal spirit.

"I believe in the justice of the struggle," Clemente whispered. "But we have been divided——"

"Yes," the chorus of men responded, "we have been divided."

"Each man lived in his own world! " Clemente's voice rose.

"Cada cabeza es un mundo——" old Manuel nodded.

"Now we must reconcile those two ideas," Clemente sought for words to express the trembling in his soul. "On the one hand we know that each man lives in his own universe, and each one of us understands the loneliness of that universe of the mind. Who has not felt that tristeza? " The men nodded, and he continued. "But we do not have to live in that aloneness, no. Long ago our people built bridges across that wide chasm and empty space that separates us from our brothers, and by the gods sacred command they called this soul of the people *el alma de la raza!* That bond unites us all, it is the holy sacrament of the new movement, it is a universal brotherhood! "

The men shifted uneasily and craned forward to hear the man speak. Many of them had believed that Clemente could be their leader, but they did not know why they felt that way, now as he found words to express himself he seemed a man possessed.

"——Universal brotherhood! " Lalo spat. He felt uneasy.

"The space between us can be bridged, a bond can unite us all! If we are to survive as a people, and if we are not to become like the americano, then the soul of the people must rise above that hell of individual alienation! Each man and woman must give up his movida——"

"Wait a minute! " Lalo interrupted. "You're telling us to give up our survival. I work my movidas to feed my family and keep a

147

roof over their heads! I know how to cheat the welfare people, I know how to trade stamps for things I need, I know the way the barrio lives and where I can pick up an extra dollar to keep my family from starving. If I give that up, who in hell's going to support me? "

Clemente bowed his head. "I understand what you say, but don't you realize how mere survival drains our energy. Don't you see that as long as we work only for our own little gain that we remain strangers to each other, and we violate the sacred trust of our fathers, el alma de la raza——"

"Bullshit! " Lalo growled. He had felt Clemente's spell and the allegiance it was drawing from the men, so he fought to regain control. "You try telling that son-a-ma-biche foreman that your soul is the same as his and he'll laugh in your face! Sure, he's raza, but he's a pinche lambe, and he don't understand any of this nice, flowery stuff you're talking about! He's looking out for himself, and that's what we should do! "

" ¡Andale! " Héctor slapped his back. "I agree with Lalo. Sure, my father and my grandfathers spoke about el alma de la raza, that was fine in their time, but people don't give a shit about things like that anymore! It don't buy beans or pay the rent! Now it's dog eat dog, and dogs make war! It's war, I say! " He cried excitedly and his eyes bulged with hatred.

Some of the men nodded, the others moved nervously. They stole glances at each other, checking to ascertain who would go if war was voted. Bad blood stirred in their veins.

"My God," Clemente groaned, "we have forgotten. It was planned this way to keep us down, and it has worked——" He turned to Crispín, but the old man sat motionless, listening.

"——What is this bond you speak of? " One of the men asked softly.

"I don't know——" Clemente shook his head. He felt confused, his self-doubt returned to gnaw at him. He asked himself, how can I advise the men to give up their movidas when I am supported by my daughters? The thought made him sad and he sighed.

"How will the soul of our people change the way things are? " Lalo challenged him. "How can the soul bend steel, how can it get our jobs back? "

"I don't know——" Clemente moaned crestfallen.

"Well, I know! " Lalo leaped in front of him and shouted. "We take our destiny in our hands! We strike! Strike! Strike! We die burning down their temples of injustice! We beat them into the ground and prepare to go to hell with them! "

It was what the men had been waiting for. Their nerves were raw with the frustration of waiting. Anything was better than sitting and listening to endless arguments.

" ¡Huelga! " They returned the call. "Strike now! "

"Wait! " Clemente shouted and stood in front of the storm at its flood. "I agree, I am with you to strike down injustice! But that is only a part of the total movement! It must be more than that! It must be a rekindling of the fire of our soul, a new awareness of——"

"Fire! " Someone picked up the word, "Chávez said fire! Burn! "

"Now you're talking, Chávez! " Lalo shouted and grabbed Clemente. "We'll burn down everything! "

A great cheer went up as the men rushed out of the hut and into the street.

"No! No! " Clemente tried to stop them. "That's not what I meant! You didn't listen——" But the screaming men rushed by him like a full arroyo when the water has crested and the flood rumbles with uncontrolled fury. The men did not hear him; only Crispín remained at his side.

Lalo and Héctor led the men up the street. Torches were lit, and the cry echoed down the barrio that the time had come. The ranks of the marching workers swelled as they moved down the street, joined by many of the people of the barrio.

Shouts of " ¡Viva la raza! " mixed into the sound of marching feet.

" ¡Justicia para la gente! "

"Down with the tyranny of the shops! " The people shouted.

Gasoline cans with rag fuses appeared. Men armed themselves with boards, whatever they could pick up to fight the spontaneous winter war. Some of the women carried their babies and were surrounded by children as wives marched by their husbands. The men from Lalo's faction openly carried guns and shouted to the workers to arm themselves.

"The time has come! Take up arms! " they shouted.

"Burn the shops! "

The waiting was over. The cry spread down the barrio and the people came running down side streets and alleys, like rivulets fed by the storm of waiting they flowed into the maelstrom that rumbled down Barelas Road. Like the roaring chocolate waters of spring-tide the crowd hit the yard's chain link fence and crumpled it. By that time la Llorona wailed on barrio streets.

The first building the enraged workers came upon as they spread across the yards was the signalman's old shack, and they overturned it and set fire to it. The dry walls of the old boxcar quickly caught fire. The workers cheered as the hot fire roared up and illuminated the night. Showers of sparks popped from the dry tinder. The people cheered. It had been so easy to start the fire; now months of indecision and of despair would be undone as quickly as the old shack. The men turned to move in other directions but by that time the police that moved in behind them had cordoned them off. The wail of la Llorona changed to a dry, garbled static, which like the dry voice of death called to be appeased. The men in blue answered by opening fire.

The first shots were like the cracking and popping of the burning wood. Two workers fell and those near them thought they had tripped; then a woman screamed as one of the hungry bullets stung her face. She touched the searing burn and when she looked at her hand the firelight glistened on her blood. She screamed again and the workers turned to face the second volley. Against the dancing fire the people were easy targets. Before the people could disperse two more had fallen, and when the confusion had abated many others lay crippled on the cinder gravel of the yards.

Next morning the city was in an uproar. The state police had been called to protect the shops and the governor threatened to call out the national guard. The morning paper carried the headline, RADICALS STRIKE NATIONS LIFELINE, and the story beneath it blamed the burning and looting on the communist strikers. The editorial damned the instigators of the wildcat strike and called for immediate and harsh prosecution of the strikers. None of the strikers grievances were listed; instead there was a picture of Kirk shaking hands with a railroad spokesman. He was quoted as saying that only a few, dissident men were responsible for the burning and that the majority of the workers and the community were in support of his union.

CHAPTER FIFTEEN

Clemente sneaked through the alley and entered Mannie's store through the back door. There were no customers. Mannie was at the counter, wistfully looking out into the tense, deserted street. His wife and daughter were on their hands and knees, scrubbing the empty aisles. The daughter was in the last months of her pregnancy, but worn looking and thin. It was said her husband beat her, and so she returned to her parents. It was a big disappointment to el Super. The plans he had for future business connections fell through, and he was the object of ridicule of many of the same people he had sought to influence. He blamed his daughter for his bad luck and treated her badly.

Clemente surveyed the quiet scene and motioned to Mannie. El Super almost fell backward when he turned and saw Clemente.

"¡Tata poderoso! " He cried and hurried towards Clemente. "Hombre, but what are you doing here? "

"I need to talk to you——" Clemente answered. The woman and her daughter looked at him suspiciously.

"To talk with me? " El Super squealed. "Every policeman in the city is looking for you, and you come to talk to me! " He laughed nervously and looked at his wife and daughter. They stood dumbfounded, looking at Clemente.

"——I, I should call the police! " El Super threatened.

"Hear me out first," Clemente held him, "then do what you will."

"Hear you out! " El Super shook nervously. "Do you realize you've cost me a whole day's business? That's right, not a single person has been in the store today? The streets are empty, the barrio seems dead, and it's all because of the trouble you caused last night! "

"I have not made trouble for any man," Clemente answered

him.

"You incited them to loot and burn! "

"No," Clemente shook his head. "I don't have that power over them . . ."

"They consider you their leader! The rumor is that they're waiting for you to give the command again and there will be more burning, more destruction! They say there are arms stored in the barrio, and that the men are waiting for a message from you to fight again. The entire barrio is barricaded, ready to explode! " He glanced furtively at his wife. He didn't know what to do.

He turned to Clemente. "——They call you a messiah, a leader of the people." His body trembled with an anxious laughter. "You the leader? Last month you were drinking yourself to sleep in the alleys of the barrio, the dogs of the alley were your only companions. How can you be the leader——"

"That is what I came to talk to you about." Clemente stepped forward. "Listen, I don't have much time, so please listen carefully. The future of the people may depend on it. It is true the police are looking for me, but that is only because they need a scapegoat. Last night they killed innocent men, and now they want to make the world believe there is a plot against the government in this poor barrio; they want to shift the attention of the papers to me and cover up the dirt the strike is exposing. In your heart you understand that! " His voice cracked like a whip and his steady gaze made el Super wince.

"I did not advocate violence last night," he continued, "that is not the path I am seeking. But the men mistook what I said, because that is what they wanted to hear. It has been a long winter for them, a cold winter full of misery and poverty, and it was natural for them to strike back and burn those forms they see as forces which keep them oppressed. Yes, I feel responsible, because I am not an educated man I do not know how to choose my words wisely, and because of me two men died—— The burden of grief is as heavy as the sin of Judas——"

El Super shuddered. The man's passion cut through his guts. "What do you want of me? " he asked.

"The men need a leader! " Clemente said and reached out and grabbled the startled storekeeper by the collar. "Without someone to take the reins, what happened last night will be repeated. You

152

said yourself the barrio is like a volcano before it blows into the sky. But if that happens we will only lose more men, there will be more deaths. You must speak to the men, you must be that leader! "

"Me! " El Super gasped and broke away. "You are crazy, Chávez, crazy——"

"You say that because the idea frightens you," Clemente said, "But you know as well as I do that you are the only man in the barrio that has a voice at City Hall! The police will listen to you! You can go and talk to them and that will relieve the tension of the confrontation, otherwise the town will go up in flames and you will see rioting as you have never seen before. Reason with the police, have them free the men that were arrested last night, they are family men for the most part but they suffer the sentence of revolutionaries. That is stupid! You know there was no looting last night. One, old boxcar was burned and the men are charged with arson of government property, and there is further threat that they will be indicted for planning to overthrow the government—— It's crazy! All they wanted was to demonstrate their plight, to act for the human rights that are theirs——"

"I can't do anything about what happened," el Super mumbled.

"You can speak out! " Clemente shouted. "You can use your influence at City Hall to help the people! "

"All right, I have listened to you, Chávez, now you listen to me! " El Super shouted angrily; the instincts that had made him a wealthy man flared up as he felt his self preservation threatened. "What makes you think I want to help the people! "

It was Clemente's turn to be surprised. "But they are your people——"

"They're nobody's people! " El Super shouted. "They are the worst of mankind, suddenly turning on the hand that has fed them for so long! Ungrateful scum, marijuanos, petty thieves, winos, leeches who live off welfare, prostitutes, wife-beaters! They're nobody's people! Why should I help them? " He shouted and gritted his teeth.

Clemente shrugged. "They are in need because they are oppressed. Walk among them, as I have, and their enslavement will touch your heart. What greater good could there be in a man's life than to lift the oppression that destroys them, what greater honor is there? "

"And lose all this? " El Super waved his arm. He laughed. "Forgive me, Chávez, but before, I thought that you were merely a crazy fool, now I know that you are mad. You can keep your honor, I will not trade it for the things that it has taken me a lifetime to acquire——"

"But you don't have to lose everything to help the people," Clemente insisted.

"Ha! That tells me how little you know about business! " El Super shook his head as if to pity Clemente. "Look, I control a large part of this barrio because I control one thing, *credit*. That's right, it's that simple. Credit is the lifeline, the blood that turns the wheels. In Barelas I control it, but out there, well, out there are bigger animals, and they in turn control my credit. It doesn't matter how good a businessman I am, if they cut off my credit I am dead, the barrio's dead, nothing grows without the green blood of the dollar. Now, how long do you think it would take the banks to cut off my credit if I joined a group of communists like you? They'd do it like this! " He snapped his fingers.

"Then you will not help——" Clemente groaned. His knees felt weak and he shuddered. He had counted on the businessman to ease the tensions that threatened to engulf the barrio.

"No! " El Super shook his head. "Now you must leave! It would not look good for me if the police found you here . . ."

"Is there anything that would make you change your mind? " Clemente asked.

El Super laughed. "Yes, if I thought I could make a profit in this struggle of yours, I would join . . . But no," he added, "There is no money to be made from poor people—— And there's something else," he said and looked at Clemente. "Suppose, just suppose I joined the cause and we won our struggle, eh, what then? For awhile, Clemente, only for awhile the people would carry me on their shoulders and call me their leader . . . But then the ugly heads of envy would rise around me, and like poisonous snakes this green envidia would strike at me. Yes, I've seen it happen too often, a man rises above his level and soon there's someone there to trip him, to make him fall . . ." He looked at the haggard figure in front of him and he pitied Clemente. The man was sick, that was easy to see, his clothes were dirty and tattered, and now he had to move from house to house in the barrio to keep ahead of the law. He shook his head and said, "I feel sorry for you, Clemente . . . Your faith is so pure and simple it is frightening. The people will follow you, the rabble is easily aroused, and now there is blood in the air and shouts for vengeance . . . perhaps you will accomplish your goal. But later, in the end, heed what I tell you, they will turn on you. Envidia will rear its green head, you will be denounced——"

Clemente shrugged. "I trust my people," he said simply.

"Yes, I know, and that is why I cannot understand you," el Super shook his head, "Because I cannot understand this abounding faith you have in the rabble. Perhaps they will keep their faith in you, but still there will be other leaders who will snap at your heels like mad dogs . . . It's all the same, in the end la envidia will destroy and take away whatever sweetness there might have been to the struggle . . ."

Clemente turned and walked away. For a week he eluded the police by staying constantly on the move. The barrio was a friendly place to him and everywhere there were people willing to take him in, and it was a foreign maze to the searchers, but after a week the illness returned and he had to seek medical help. He was weak and feverish again when Roberto took him to the hospital, and before he could be treated he was handcuffed and thrown in jail. It was a few days before the people of the barrio could raise the bail so by the time he was freed he was sick from a racking cold and his throat was so sore he could barely speak. Still he vowed to continue the fight from the courthouse steps, and the people cheered and gathered around him. For him there was no turning back.

CHAPTER SIXTEEN

Pato groaned and cursed his luck. He looked at the pimple growing on the tip of his nose and swore he was going to kill himself.

"What's the matter? " Jason asked.

"I'm cursed! " he moaned. "Oh, God, why me? "

"Got the chatos? " Pete asked.

"Too much Marlene! " Dickie laughed. "He's got something for sure! "

"I wish it was that simple! " Pato shook his head sadly and looked in the mirror.

They were showering after swimming at the Y and Willie twirled his wet towel and popped Pato, but Pato didn't fight back. "Go away mocoso," he barely responded.

"Come on, Pato, let's go get some burgers at the Red Ball," Chelo tried to cheer him up, but Pato wasn't dressing. He sat dripping on the wooden bench and continued to stare in the mirror.

"I'm going to kill myself," he moaned.

"That bad, huh? "

"Try not eating," Willie offered, "bet you change your mind! "

"What's the matter, ése? " Jason asked again.

"He couldn't undo Marlene's brassiere, and that ruined his big macho reputation! " Willie laughed.

"You really going to kill yourself? " Pete asked, his analytical curiosity already thinking of a method.

" ¡Me la rayo por me jefita! " Pato swore on his mother's honor.

"Why don't you do it by playing chicken with Johnny from Sanjo, the way James Dean did it in the movie——"

" ¡A toda madre! " Dickie agreed. "We haven't had anyone play chicken since last summer when Lizard chickened out Borrego. They went on the high, narrow dirt road that runs along the canal, so either way one of them would lose. If they stayed on they would have rammed their cars into each other doing fifty or sixty, and if one of them chickened out then he wound up at the bottom of the embankment. Anyway, Borrego chickened out and swerved at the last minute. He was all right, but they say he dirtied his pants——"

They laughed. They had heard about the crazy game.

"They call me crazy," Willie said, "but you won't find me doing anything stupid like that! "

"Well, after that Lizard was a goddamned hero. He had all the chicks he wanted. Why, man, they lined up just to drive up to the west mesa with him! "

"Yeah, I'm convinced that's the only way to do it, Pato," Pete nodded assuringly. "That way you not only get even with Johnny for making a fool out of you in front of Falsie, you'll also die a hero."

"Yeah," Pato nodded, "maybe you're right. I really had it made with Falsie before he showed up. I had her lined up to find out if those big things are real or not, and then he came along——"

"He wanted to play chicken then," Willie reminded him.

"I couldn't," Pato shrugged it off, "my car wasn't insured——"

"Forget about insurance," Dickie laughed, "when those two cars come dragging down on each other and nobody chickens out, the only insurance you need is upstairs."

"They might even make a movie out of your life," Pete said.

"Yeah," Pato nodded. He would be a hero, the chicks would be crying at his funeral. He'd be the talk around school for a week. He'd go out laughing, like a real man, and Falsie would be sorry she hadn't given in while she had the chance.

"Yeah," that's the best way they all agreed.

"I'd like to be your manager, if you decide to go ahead with it," Pete said solemnly and put his hand on Pato's shoulder.

"Thanks, Pete," Pato answered bravely, but he was already beginning to have second thoughts about the whole thing. Sure the chicks would be crying as he lay handsome-as-hell in his coffin, but what the hell good was that if he was dead.

"Well, we're ready, let's go." They had finished dressing.

157

Pato was still looking in the mirror. "I've tried everything," he moaned, "nothing works."

"Before we go," Jason paused, "will you tell us what it is? What's the problem? "

"Can't you see! " Pato cried and turned around. He pointed at the red, juicy pimple on his nose.

"A pimple! That's all? " Jason gasped.

"It's ruined me——" Pato slumped on the bench. "I'll never be able to look another girl in the face——"

"Goodbye Falsie! " Willie sang, "We'll never know if you were for reals! " They left, leaving behind a brooding and dejected Pato.

They ran into the street, wrestling with each other to keep away the biting cold. The Y was one of the few places they could go without money, and after a swim they always felt good. Even the cold could not hold back their laughter and shouts of joy.

"Hey! ¡Ese, ése vato loco, tirilón, cabrón, órale, que tal! ¡Aviéntate! ¡Déjate cai! " They strung chuco words to crazy music and challenged the streets.

"We're from Barelas! Move aside, ése! "

"We'll take on any mutha! "

"Any barrio! "

"The whole world! "

" ¡Orale! " They bopped down the windy streets, shadow boxing, punching at each other, feeling good and high. "Let's go to the dance at the Center tonight! "

"Can't, Pato's got the monthlies! "

"Wish we had another car——"

"Did you hear about Cindy? She had to drop outta school. She was blown up and beginning to show."

"You got some of that, huh Jason? " one of the cuates asked.

"Nah, not me," Jason answered. He knew the cuates had started the rumor at school that he had knocked up Cindy.

"Her old man had the principal replaced because he couldn't come up with the vato that took advantage of his little girl——"

"Advantage hell! Cindy can handle anyone. Wish it'a been me! "

"I'm betting it was Jason," one of the cuates grinned. "We know she had the hots for him last summer."

158

"Screw off! " Jason said angrily. He normally didn't mind the jiving, but he was worried that the rumor would get to Cristina.

"I'll bet a coke it wasn't! " Chelo took the bet.

"A coke and a burger! " The cuate answered. "And you have to prove it! "

"I already have," Chelo smiled. "I asked Lorraine. She's been working in the nurses office at school, and she saw the date the doctor put down. It was way after the party . . . by that time Jason had met Cristina and you know damn well he hasn't messed with another chavala since he met her! "

"Yeah," the others agreed and looked at the cuates.

"He could'of sneaked back! " one of them protested.

"Yeah, he could'of, and that's what Cindy wanted. She chased him for weeks after that, and she never knew why Jason turned her down. She was madder than hell, so she made it with someone else, right? "

"All right! " Willie slapped Chelo on the back.

"So how come she put the finger on Jason? "

"She was jealous, right? If she couldn't get Jason she figured she'd break him and Cristina up. You know the way women are, man . . ."

"You can't trust 'em! " Willie nodded. "A woman who gets jealous like that'll do anything."

"Love them and leave them, that's my motto."

"Mota? Treat them like mota . . . get high on them, then vámonos! "

" ¡Orale! " they shouted.

"Innocent as hell until you get a little——"

"Then they've got you, de los huevos! "

"Yeah."

"Gotta let them know who's the boss, right away. If she steps outta line, watch out! Truchas! It's the end! "

"Yeah, you can't let your old lady run your life. I've seen guys that are caught like that, and man I feel sorry for them. It's not going to be that way in my family! "

"Yeah! "

They sauntered into the small cafe, welcoming the greasy warmth and crowding into booths. Conio, the old man who owned the cafe, knew they wouldn't order anything so he didn't move

159

from behind the counter. They were still feeling wild and making a lot of noise, so the older vatos told them to be quiet, then they settled down and listened to the small talk. The talk centered around the strike and the lack of work.

"Work is scarce, all right," Freddie said, "I swear there's not one pinche jale in this town! "

"I was lucky," Eloy said. "I went to work with my old man. He has a trade, something I could get into . . . I pity the vatos whose jefitos work at the shops; there's nothing to pass on there . . ."

"I wish they'd settle this friggin' thing one way or the other! " Phil cursed. "I'm tried of the law breathin' down my neck everytime I turn around."

"They'd settle it if they could get Kirk and his pack of lambes out of office," Bernie said. He turned to Jason. "How's your old man, Jason? "

"He's better," Jason answered.

"Damn, he sure gave it to them. He had them chasing around here for a week . . . they never would of caught him if he hadn't gotten sick. I'm glad somebody finally stood up——"

"Yeah, but what did it get him, man? " Phil asked. "He's only out on bail, ése, and when that trial comes they're going' to stick it to him! "

"Yeah, but he had the huevos to do something! "

"What? They tore down a fence and burned a shack, got two of Lalo's boys killed and the rest busted! They gotta do something else! There's got to be a way! "

"Well he's the only leader they have," Freddie defended him, "I think he could clear up the whole thing if only everybody got behind him."

"Nah, nah," Phil disagreed, "you gotta get somebody in there whose got an education, somebody who knows all their movidas. Without an education you're a nobody. I know, ése, every jale I apply for and the first question they ask for is, 'Got an education, boy? ' "

"It's getting so you have to have a high school diploma to work as a janitor, to sweep floors, to empty a trash can——"

"How about el Super? "

"Well, he knows the score, baby, but do you think he'll help? Nah. He learned how the business works, okay, and in one word it's money. As long as your're in control of the bank's money and credit, man, you're the boss man."

"——How about Father Cayo? "

"Why, man! " Phil laughed, "you know he ain't gonna rock the boat! What do you think, Jessie? " He prodded Jessie. Jessie had been in Korea and he had gone crazy in the war, now he hung around the barrio and did nothing.

"You gotta take care of number one, yeah! " Jessie grinned, "you gotta take care of numero uno——" He looked like an old man in army green.

"Okay, suppose we agree with Phil's idea that we gotta get somebody that's educated, now who in the hell do you know from the barrio that's got an education? I don't know anyone, do you? "

"Yeah, there's a few, but they've all moved away . . ."

"All you need is unity! " Freddie argued. "If everybody got together just once, why man they'd shut down the friggin' city! Look, who picks up the garbage, who does city maintenance, who does the back-breaking work, huh? We do! You let people lie in their garbage for a few days and you stop them from going places and I bet they'll come up with more money . . ."

"Yeah, if we go out the whole show comes to a stop, doesn't it? "

"Bull! They'd bring in scab labor! "

"Nah, man, not if everybody went out all at once! "

"How you gonna get that to happen, ése? " Phil asked sarcastically. They looked at him and shook their heads. They didn't know how.

"I guess that's the answer Jason's father is trying to find," Eloy said thoughtfully.

"And it's not easy . . . Even our own people are split. Some are for the workers cause, and some aren't . . . The day after the burning the radio had a talk show, and a lot of people called in denouncing Clemente . . ."

"They're afraid——"

"People don't want to rock the boat; everybody's got his own thing going and they don't want to be bothered about the workers' cause . . ."

"And that's just what Jason's father told the strikers. Each person has to give up his movidas and get behind the bigger——"

"Hell no! " Phil interrupted. "I ain't giving up my movidas! That's survival! Take care of numero uno first, right Jessie? "

"Gotta watch out for number one, yeah, that's what the war taught me. Watch out for yourself, stay alive! " Jessie laughed crazily.

Conio told them not to get Jessie started. "——Don't make him talk, you know he gets sick every time he remembers——" But they didn't pay attention and they asked him about Korea.

"Hey, Jessie, you joined the Marines! Weren't the Marines a team? Didn't you join to fight for your country? "

"Shit no," Jessie trembled, "I didn't join for no country, I joined to even the score! My two carnales, Jerry and Billie, they joined before me and they both got killed in Korea, and so I joined to even the score. I did, too! I killed more commies than you can count, yeah! I joined the guys that would teach me how to kill, and they did! Then they gave me a Silver Star for it and said I was a good Marine, but I did it for my brothers! "

He started shaking and Eloy had to hold the match so Jessie could light his cigarette. Conio tried to get Jessie to stop but once Jessie started talking he was possessed, he couldn't stop until he told his story. The only thing Conio could do was go to the back room and bring Jessie a bottle of wine to drink, at least that way he wouldn't go crazy and get the shaking fits that usually put him back in the VA hospital.

"How many did you kill, Jessie? "

"A lot, yeah, I killed a lot of mutha commies. I lost count, man. At first I was counting. I'd fire a spurt with the BAR and I'd see three or four go down, and I'd count them. And I'd throw a grenade and count the ones that went down, but after awhile it didn't matter anymore, I lost count. They just kept pouring over the barbed wire perimeter, yeah, they came in waves—and I remember, it was a cold day, yeah, it was a cold mutha day. I kept looking up at the dull, gray sky, thinking it was gonna snow. God, how I wished it would snow! "

He paused and took a long drink, and he stopped trembling.

"——At first it was what I wanted, yeah, 'Come on you muthers! ' I was yelling at them, 'Come and get it! ' It was what I wanted, to even the score for my brothers. But after awhile it didn't make sense anymore, they just kept coming and I kept killing them, until I was surrounded by dead bodies. I ran out of ammo, and all of my buddies were either dead or they'd pulled back, but I stayed, yeah, and I was taking them on with my bayonet! I was red with blood, and I kept looking up at that cold, empty sky and wishing it would snow, God, how I prayed for snow, beautiful white, clean snow that would come down and cover everything."

He was crying now, remembering everything in detail, smelling warm, sticky human blood on his hands again, remembering their eyes as they died, living in the vacuous day whose time was fixed forever in his mind. He was crying and drinking wine and telling his story because he was cursed to tell it.

The cafe was very silent.

"——I lost my bayonet. I shoved it in some cabrón, but I didn't twist it, so it stuck. I was too tired, yeah, I remember the man going down with my pig-sticker in him, and so after that I fought them with my bare hands, yeah. I ripped at their throats like an animal, knee-deep in bodies and blood, I scratched out eyes, I tore at flesh—even when the squad regrouped and came back to my position I was still killing like a madman. I couldn't tell the difference between my buddies and the commies, I just wanted to kill everything in sight. They had to hold me down, yeah, hold me and talk to me until I calmed down, and when I saw that goddamned mess I cried. Yeah, I cried like a baby and I prayed to God for it to snow and cover all our sins——"

He gulped down the last of the wine and took a deep drag of his cigarette. Then he laughed.

"They gave me a Silver Star for what I did, yeah! They called me a hero, I shook hands with generals, and I didn't have to fight anymore, 'cause I'd done my job well. And when they brought me back they took me to the White House and I met the president, and he patted me on the back and said I was a good man and my country was proud of me. Yeah, proud of me. And when I got back here they declared Jessie Martinez day, and they had a big parade for me. They took me around to all the schools, hell I didn't know what was happening, and they told all of the little kids that I was a hero——"

He shook his head slowly then laid it on his folded arms.

"Oh God, it was a goddamn mess——" He cried.

"Korea——"

"Yeah."

"It must have been rough——"

They paused and reflected on the war and what it had meant, and the cafe was silent except for the sound of sizzling burger patties frying on the burner.

"A lot of vatos from the barrio went, and they died there."

"It wasn't even our war, I mean, it's a long way off. But we went."

"Yeah."

"Why? "

"To save the world from communism, that's what the priest said. Hell, I felt like joining myself, but I was too young. I'd leave mass on Sunday after one of those sermons and I really felt like joining up! "

"Maybe we saved the world from communism, but it didn't do us any good. What good is saving the world if you can't even get a job, huh? Our carnales fought and died there, and we got our heroes like Jessie, but that don't cut no ice with the man. All he says is drop outta school and join the army, we'll find another war for you to fight! "

"Yeah, you talk to these vatos and they tell you that nothing changed after the war, nothing. Prices went up, that's all, and jobs got scarcer, and we're still in the same pobreza. The streets are the same, the junk's the same——"

"When my brother Santiago went to war the only thing I can remember is my mother crying and praying," Phil said.

"Pobrecitas las madrecitas, they're the ones who suffer——"

"You can say that again," Phil nodded. "Man, I don't think I'll ever forget the way she cried when we got the letter saying Santiago had been killed. It seemed like he'd only been gone a month—— I can still remember the way he looked dressed up in his uniform, his girl was with him and we had a big fiesta at the house. Everybody was happy, and then just a month later all that's left is a couple of dogtags, and his picture on my mother's cómoda, right next to the statue of la Virgen de Guadalupe. It's strange, but there are only two things on that huge dresser: my mother's altar with all her saints and candles, and the pictures of the men of our family who have been to war. There's a picture of my grandfather, dressed in a World War One uniform, my jefito who was in the Normandy invasion, my uncle who died in Bataan, and then Santiago, Korea——"

"I remember Santiago," Freddie said, "it was my first day at La Washa and this big gabacho jumped me—— Santiago took care of me, he always took care of the vatos from Barelas. He was like a hero to us——"

"Yeah, and all the heroes died in Korea——"

"Except Jessie."

They looked at Jessie. He was almost asleep, glassy-eyed with the wine he drank too fast. His head nodded softly to the rhythm of the jukebox.

"You know, I remember Jessie before he went to Korea, he used to box in the Golden Gloves every year, and he always won. The guy wouldn't drink, he wouldn't smoke anything, everybody looked up to him, but when he came back from the war, well, he wasn't the same anymore."

"He stands on street corners, talking to himself."

"My old man says it's because of the memories he has to live with, pobre vato——"

"Come on, you vatos! " Eloy interrupted, "Let's get off that depressing stuff! ¡Una tristeza de la chingada! " He dropped a quarter in the jukebox. "What I want is a job, man, a jale so I can settle down. I'm tired of spending every night en la peda! "

They listened thoughtfully because it was new to hear Eloy talk about that. All of the older vatos of the barrio seemed to lead an exciting life, and yet here was one of their leaders talking about settling down.

"I know what you mean, daddy-o, my jefita is after my ass too. '¡Vagamundo, sin vergüenza! Get married,' she tells me. '¡Haste hombre, como tu papá! ' " Freddie nodded in agreement.

"Yeah," Phil agreed, "La parranda gets old after awhile . . ."

"Yeah," they agreed. Whoring and drinking did get old, and even the bonds of the gang begin to crack as they grow older and begin to think of settling down.

"Pinche agüite, ése," Eloy cursed. He stood up and looked at Jessie. "I'm tired of hanging around here," he said as he looked around the small, greasy cafe. Suddenly everything was too small and pressing in on him and he felt like leaving and running in the cold air.

So one by one they filed out, leaving behind a time of life, and each one walked alone down the dark streets of the barrio. Their restless blood hustled them with the torment of their sperm and drove them to seek warmer nests. In the future they would return to the Red Ball to talk awhile with Conio and to reminisce over a Wimpy burger, but it would never be as it had once been. Around them younger vatos would be ruling the booths and tables, talking about the drunks they threw, and bragging about the women they knew.

CHAPTER SEVENTEEN

Christmas came and the bright lights and the festivity of preparation helped to dispel the gloom that had settled over the barrio. For a week the workers and the police guards had kept each other at bay in an uneasy truce, then suddenly there was a lessening of tension as the festive season came upon them. The guard forces around the yards were reduced and the strikers pulled back from their activity to regroup. A strange but welcomed peace fell over the barrio. People began to move in the streets that had been empty, and bright lights sparkled on the sheet of water the winter rain had left on the asphalt.

Los vatos moved restlessly and randomly up Barelas Road; they paused in front of the bar and listened to the mariachi music. Two nice-looking pachucas passed by and the vatos ate them up with their macho eyes, calling after them, " ¡Ay, que cosas hace Dios! " The pachucas laughed and walked on; one of them teased back: " ¡Si no fueras tan mocoso te llevara a casa! "

The gang howled and punched at Willie, and he lifted his baggy pants and wiped at his nose. "Ah," he said, "I got a cold . . ."

"You're always running, Willie——"

They walked on, stopping in front of the Red Ball. They looked through the steaming window.

"Anybody got money for Wimpies? "

"Nah."

"Shit . . ." They moved away. At Ruppes they remembered last summer and the night they had gone to las Golondrinas. It seemed like a long time ago.

"We don't do things like that anymore," Dickie said.

"We don't get together that often . . ."

"Yeah, seems like what's happened here has broken up a lot of things . . ."

"We're just growing up," Willie said, but nobody paid attention.

"Well, you dragged me out here," Pato shivered, "so what do you wanna do tonight? "

"Too cold and wet to do anything, like we did last summer . . ."

"We could go to the Y and shoot pool——"

"Ah man, I'm tired of that shit."

"Any parties? "

"Nah, nothing . . ."

"They're decorating the church for Christmas," Jason offered.

"Any chicks? " Pato asked.

"Yeah, Cristina said there was going to be a few girls there . . . Falsie will be there," he kidded Pato.

" ¡Orale! " Pato livened up, "I'm for that! " He looked at the others and they agreed.

"Come on! " Willie complained, "For crying out loud! Who wants to spend Saturday night in church? "

"I do," Pato answered, "if there's chicks there! " They laughed.

"Bull! I can think of better things." He turned to Jason. "Why you wanna have anything to do with the church after what the priest and that gang of crooks done to your old man? "

"What? " Pete asked.

"Everybody in Barelas knows about it," Willie wiped his nose, "they tried to buy Jason's father out——"

"Who? "

"Who else, dummy! " Willie jerked his head sideways after blowing into the gutter. "The políticos, that's who! They got together with the shop bosses and they all agreed to get rid of Jason's dad . . . they're afraid of him cause the people were looking up to him like a leader, and they thought he was getting too powerful . . ."

"How do you know? " Pete asked.

"My father overheard everything," Willie answered. "He was in the alley behind the church one night, and that's what he heard. He told me he heard a bunch of men arguing in the priest's room, so he peeped in the window, and all these rich cats were sitting around smoking cigars and drinking wine, the wine the priest keeps which is supposed to be the blood of Christ. They were drinking it, and they were planning to get rid of Chávez, because he's got over half the workers organized, something that's never

168

happened before, and the way he speaks now he's getting all the people on the strikers side——"

"You swear your old man told you this, Willie? "

"And he didn't just make it up cause he don't like priests? "

"I swear to God," Willie said. "And my jefito ain't ever lied to me. He may be a dog-killer, like you say, and he may gather old Christ-bread out of the alley cause we gotta eat, but he ain't no liar. Ask Jason, he knows him——" Jason nodded.

"Well, what did they do? " Dickie asked.

"The shop bosses put a lot of money on the table, and the políticos added to the pile, and then they said, 'Get rid of that man. He's a trouble-maker, and no good for any of our businesses. It wouldn't look right for us to get involved, but he's your own kind, so get rid of him——' "

"And our people took it? " Pete winced.

"Yeah," Willie nodded, "they took the money to buy him out. There's a little bit of Judas in all of us," he added philosophically.

"Did he take it? " One of the cuates asked.

"What the hell's the matter with you! " Chelo cried angrily, "Do you think for one moment that Jason's dad can be bought? No, not of all men, not him. Tell them what happened, Willie."

"They won't believe it," Willie shrugged. "They'll just say I'm crazy——"

"Tell us, Willie," Pato begged, "we'll listen! "

"Well, they waited until they could find Chávez alone, except they didn't know that by now the men are guarding him, taking care of him, so there are witnesses. The businessmen, with Father Cayo and el Super as their leaders, went to Chávez, and they made him the offer. They told him the pile of money was his if he got out of town, left for good and forgot the strike. They told him there was enough money there to take care of him the rest of his life. And they also told him that the law was on their side, and that the law knew that Lalo kept guns and that it was only a matter of time before he was arrested. Then it would be so easy to arrest Jason's dad along with him, and send him away for good. They told him to take the money, that it was the best way out for all of them——"

"And what did Jason's father do? " Dickie asked.

"They say he was very angry at first, that he twisted with anger at the insult, but then, they say, he just laughed at them, and he told them he pitied them because they were weak men and did not know that honor can't be bought. Anyway, that's when the big chingadera happened. They say Chávez extended his hand, and el Super smiled because he thought Chávez was going to take the money. He jumped forward and offered the bagful of money, and when Chávez touched it the whole thing went up in flames. Pouff! Just like that! El Super screamed and dropped the burning money. They tried to stamp out the flames, but they wouldn't die until the money was in ashes, and when they saw what had happened, they turned and ran——"

"Damn," one of the cuates scratched his head, "that's kinda hard to believe, ése."

"Believe what you want."

"It wouldn't be the first time that money sent to do the devil's work turned into ashes," Chelo reminded them.

"Anyway, there were men there that saw it. They say they saw a miracle, so what can you say. To believe in a miracle you gotta have faith. Now the people have faith in Chávez, they come to hear him speak, sometimes they just reach out to touch him——"

They were at the front of the church. Pato ran up the steps and looked in. "There's all kind of women in there! " He shouted excitedly.

" ¡Vamos! " The others cried and ran up the steps to join him. Only Willie hung back. "Chale, not me," he shook his head.

Jason turned at the highest step of the temple. "Come on, Willie! "

"Nah! " Willie shouted, "not me! I ain't going in to help that bingo player. He wouldn't pray for poor, dead Henry, just cause we're poor he wouldn't say a rosary for my brother! I'll wait outside. And Jason, I wouldn't go in there after what he done against your father——"

"I'm not going in there for him," Jason tried to make him understand, "I'm going in because I promised Christina I'd help her. It's for her——"

" ¡Vamos! " The vatos shouted at the door, " ¡Andale! Come on! "

"Nah, not me," Willie sniffed and raised the collar of his jacket to ward off the cold, "I'll stick by what I believe——"

170

"All we're gonna do is mess around with the chicks! " Pato shouted.

"Yeah, and one of these days you're goin' to have to choose, just like I had to! " Willie's shout rang in the cold, damp air. He stood alone in the night, a self-declared exile from the church.

"What did he say? " Chelo asked as they rushed inside.

"I didn't hear him," Jason answered, and lied to himself.

" ¡Está loco! " Dickie added. "Don't listen to him, he's crazy! "

They splashed holy water on their foreheads and raced into the church. The fragrance of green pine and piñon filled the dimly lit church. The fresh smell of the curative trementina mixed with the stale, holy odor of the old wax of sputtering candles. Pale men and women worked to set up the manger scene of the nacimiento. A pale white Joseph and Mary knelt at the crib that held the baby Jesus. Plaster sheep and cows waited to be arranged.

It was cold inside the church. Jason shivered and thought about Willie waiting outside. He wouldn't come to the green altar of Christ because, as he insisted, Christ wasn't born in a church anyway.

"Jason! " Cristina called. She was working with the girls, stringing green boughs and red-ribbon bows. He went to help her, while the rest of the gang scattered out to help different girls.

" ¡Orale! " Pato shouted, "The men are here! Need any help? " He boasted, but he approached them cooly, letting them know that he recognized a woman's job, but letting them know he was willing to help. Some of the girls turned their noses up at his offer, they knew his reputation, others giggled. Only fat Gloria called immediately for help.

"Yeah! " She called from atop the ladder that swayed dangerously under her two hundred pounds, "Hold the ladder——"

Pato grabbed the ladder. He looked up and grinned lasciviously. "—— ¡Qué nalgotas! " The sound rumbled in his throat and his mouth dropped open. The cuates came running to look.

Jason helped Cristina string wire, the rest helped make the wreaths that would soon be hung. Their joking and laughter gave life to the tomb-silence of the church. The parents that worked on the nacimiento scene at first glanced uneasily in the direction of the noisy workers, but then they too relaxed and the work grew lighter. One woman had brought biscochitos which she unwrapped and passed around, another woman served hot coffee.

Only one woman shriveled at the sound of the merriment. She was el Super's wife. Everyone called her la Lengua because she was a mitotera, a woman who couldn't live without spreading gossip. She hissed and her tongue flicked out and lisped poison into unsuspecting ears. Idle gossip to pass the time during la visita, it was a part of la plática del barrio, and usually it passed with a ripple of laughter and no more than a startled expression, but la Lengua whispered it struck like rabies. It marked its victim, and sometimes the bite was fatal.

Mitote was her mangey dog that scampered down the dusty alleys of the barrio, leaped across fences into the backyards where women hung their wash, and suddenly turned like a voracious wolf on its victim. In the end this whimpering, pitiful dog could devour and destroy its victims because he preyed upon the weak.

It was la Lengua who had spread the gossip about doña Carlota, la vieja de don Federico, who had arthritis so bad she couldn't even pee, so she went to la sobadora whose remedy was to cover her with fresh cow dung from head to toe, and as la Lengua told the story the only thing it did for her was make her smell like a cow. After that doña Carlota was called la Caca-Vaca, and after that her entire family was called los Caca-Vacas, and later whole generations of that family would be known as los Caca-Vacas, and because they had to bear the onerous weight of that degrading name they would begin to act and think like lowly Caca-Vacas and their life's destiny was changed.

She also told the story of la señora Pacheco who was on welfare and who let her kids run around garrientos y mocosos because she used her welfare check to buy wine for the endless trek of men who came to father her endless family. The welfare worker stayed one night to catch her in her crime, and according to la Lengua la señora Pacheco invited him in, and so now he finds himself the father of a ready-made family and on the welfare he once doled out so miserly.

There were many other gossips she spread, and the reason she did it was because as a young woman she had been bitten by the scroungy dog, and she had never recovered. The bite had made her mad with the rabies of bitterness. When she was a girl she had been betrothed to a young man from one of the best families of

172

Bernalillo. He was the scion of a very influential family and destined to become governor of the state, and so a political marriage was arranged between him and the beautiful Rosa de Castillo y Cortés, la Lengua'a maiden name. Everything was settled, until one of the pícaros of the town started a rumor that Rosa was no longer a virgin. Well, the mitote spread, her fiance abandoned her, the family was dishonored. They had been gente rica, gente de razón, but they lost everything. Her father dropped his business and took to driving from barrio to barrio in a horse-drawn wagon, Rosa sitting quietly at his side, while he futilely tried to explain that his daughter's virginity was intact. And she learned that the harder one tries to explain away a rumor, the worse it gets. Inside of a year he had lost his entire fortune and his daughter withered into old-maid years. Many years later el Super came along, and recognizing a good bargain he married her because her father threw in a dowry to help el Super start his business.

Tonight Jason was the object of la Lengua's scorn. She recognized Clemente's son, and so she would get even for the embarrassment that man had caused her husband. His laughter reminded her of the cruel blows fate had dealt her. Her envy at their joy made hackles rise on her back. She growled.

"——That, that boy, that's him! " She whispered the seed of destruction in señora Sánchez's ear.

"What boy? " Señora Sánchez asked. She looked in the direction of la Lengua's nod and saw only Jason.

"You mean you don't know? " She grinned like the beguiling serpent. She knew that curiosity is the sister of mitote.

"Know what? What's there to know? "

"Shhhhh——" la Lengua hissed. "If you do not know then I will not tell you! "

"Fine," señora Sánchez smiled, "What I don't know can't hurt me——" She knew la Lengua's ways.

"All the same! " La Lengua grabbed her before she could resume her work, "If Cristina were my daughter I would not let her near that boy! "

La señora Sánchez glanced at Cristina. "Why? " she asked.

"You really do not know, poor woman." La Lengua shook her head sadly.

"But what is there to know? " la señora Sánchez insisted, "Tell me? "

La Lengua glanced around suspiciously then pulled her into the confessional. She pulled the curtain and in the dark she whispered her lies. "Do you know about Cindy, la gabachita from the Country Club, the girl who got sick with the baby? "

"Sí," la señora Sánchez nodded, "Cristina said the poor girl had to leave school——"

"Well, it was one of the boys from the barrio who got her sick! "

"No! "

"Yes, I swear by all the saints! One of the girls from school brought her to me because she was afraid of her parents and wanted to throw up the baby . . . I took her to Doña Clemencia, la sobadora who does such work for young girls without husbands, but the girl was already too far in her pregnancy! And so the girl's parents have sent her away to have the baby——"

"That has nothing to do with me," la señora Sánchez said nervously and pulled away. She was afraid of what la Lengua was alluding to.

But la Lengua clung to her and wouldn't let her move. "I do not want to be the one who brings you bad news, comadre, but for your own sake you must know. While we talked the frightened girl confessed that it was one of Clemente's sons who fathered the child! "

"No! " Señora Sánchez covered her mouth and stifled her cry.

"I swear by the Holy Cross and all the saints that those were her exact words! One of Clemente's boys! "

The shocking words made Cristina's mother gasp for breath. She stumbled out of the confessional, still shaking her head in disbelief. She didn't want to believe the story but suddenly all the allusions she had heard about the girl and Jason fell into place. One of the cuates had mentioned Jason's name in connection with the girl's pregnancy, but she had dismissed the rumor. Now Rosa swore by the holy saints that the girl had confessed to her. She felt nauseated, but when she thought of her daughter her feeling changed to one of self-protection. She reached out and pulled Cristina away from Jason's side.

"Mamá! " Cristina cried in surprise. Everyone turned at her cry. "What's the matter? What's wrong? " Her mother's fingernails cut

174

into her flesh.

"Him! " her mother shouted and pointed at Jason. " ¡Ese sin vergüenza! "

"Mrs. Sánchez——" Jason cried helplessly. He reached out for Cristina but she held her daughter back.

"No! You will never touch her again! I trusted you, and all the time you were sneaking around and . . ." She couldn't finish, but she swore by God that he would never see Cristina again. Cristina began to cry. She didn't understand what was happening.

"But what's the matter? " Jason pleaded. "Tell me what's wrong? "

"You know what you did wrong! " La Lengua leaped forward and shook her finger in Jason's face. "Everyone knows you are the father of the coyotito that mocosa gabachita went away to breed! "

"Jason, no——" Cristina gasped. She felt her knees grow weak.

"It's not true! " Jason answered, but his voice was drowned by the thundering accusation of the priest. Father Cayo had over-heard everything and now he jumped forward and shouted, "Can this filth I hear be true! " His face was red with rage; los vatos cringed and slipped out of the church. Only Chelo remained standing by Jason.

"It's true, padre," la Lengua fell to the floor, clutching at the priest's hand, "I heard it with my own ears——"

"Then you not only sinned with that girl but you confessed falsely! " The priest shouted at Jason. "And for that you are doubly damned! "

The group of men and women were shocked. They pulled together as if for protection when they heard the priest's curse, and they crossed their foreheads and looked accusingly at Jason. An old woman muttered, "Por la señal de la Santa Cruz," and made a cross in Jason's direction.

"I didn't confess falsely! " Jason defended himself. "And what this woman says isn't true! Cristina! It's not true! " he pleaded, but her mother covered her ears and drew her into the circle of women who had gathered around to assist her.

"It is true! " La Lengua insisted. "I swear by God's Holy Name, I heard it from the girl's own lips! "

"You lie! " Chelo shouted in Jason's defense. "If Cindy said

175

that she lied, and now you repeat the lie! You old bitch, everyone here should know better than to listen to your lies! "

"Chelo! " Father Cayo admonished him, "Do not follow your false friend in his evil path! At this very moment the curse of eternal damnation hangs over his head! "

"Forgive me, father," Chelo said respectfully, "but you should know that these are lies. Cindy spread the lie because she was jealous after Jason wouldn't see her anymore, and——" He looked into the priest's eyes and suddenly realized that what he said really didn't make a difference anyway, Jason was condemned, and then Chelo remembered Willie's story and understood how Jason felt.

"And, he had seen that girl! " The priest shouted.

"Yes, but——"

"And he had knowledge of her——" He turned to Jason and pointed an accusing finger, "Do you deny that? "

"I don't have to confess to you! " Jason shouted back, "I don't have to confess to any of you! You have already judged me, but I'm not guilty! "

"Out of my church! " The priest shouted and trembled with rage. "Out! You darken God's temple with your stubborn pride! You are like your father! "

"Ave María Purísima," an old woman muttered. The name of the radical Chávez was anathema to her ears.

"Vamos, Jason——" Chelo pulled him away, "it's no use, they won't listen."

"Cristina! " Jason called, but her mother wouldn't let her move.

"Don't look back! " Chelo said as he pulled Jason towards the door, but Jason heard Cristina call his name and he turned, and as he did he saw her disappear into the circle of old women that gathered around to protect her.

"Away! Away! " Father Cayo shouted hysterically.

They stumbled into the cold, clear air of the night. Willie was waiting for them.

"Chingao, what happened in there? " he asked. "The vatos came running out like the bats of hell! "

"Hell, everything got screwed up," Chelo groaned. He felt sorry for Jason, and he didn't know what to do.

"Pues, what happened? " Willie jumped up and down and

176

slapped himself with his arms to keep warm.

"Oh, that pinche ruca, la Lengua, she told everyone in there that it was Jason who screwed up Cindy! Cristina's mom had a fit, told Jason he'd never see Cristina again, and the priest got in the act and kicked us out of the church, an——"

"And what? " Willie asked.

"Damn! Isn't that enough! " Chelo cursed their bad luck.

"Is that all? " Willie asked. "You mean you're acting like the world's gonna end because the priest kicked you out of the church, and because some momma's protecting her little girl? Why shit, that ain't nothing," he smiled. Drops of cold rain splattered on his face. His eyes blinked mischievously, and he sniffed real hard to keep his mocos from dripping.

He turned to Jason. "Damn, you gotta have more faith in love than that, man, or else you're going to be like the rest of the vatos who went in there acting like big machos but who run like hell when the priest shouts." He laughed. "Nah, man, you gotta have more faith than that——"

He grinned and made them laugh. They knew he was right, and so they laughed, slowly at first then in a roar. They laughed at Willie's crazy expression and at the way he kept wiping his nose and jumping up and down to keep warm, and they laughed because already the antics of the people in the church were ludicrous. They knew that if they kept their faith and love, things would get straightened out, somehow, and so they stood in the middle of their barrio at the beginning of what already had been a long night, and they laughed in the light rain which was changing to wisps of snow.

CHAPTER EIGHTEEN

After Christmas Jason went to Cindy's home in an attempt to get her to tell Cristina the truth, but the woman who answered the door told him Cindy wasn't there and slammed the door shut.

He walked back across the frozen park towards the barrio, depressed because he couldn't see Cristina and angry because there didn't seem to be anything he could do to convince her mother that he had never been involved with Cindy; and now Cindy was gone and she had taken the truth with her.

He had tried to get in touch with Cristina through fat Gloria, but she remained obedient to her mother's wish and refused to see him. He had been frustrated in every attempt to contact her, but the separation only strengthened his love for her and renewed his resolution to see her. He had tried to talk to her at midnight mass, la misa de gallo, but she had been with her mother and would not stop to speak. He remembered that after mass his family and neighbors had gathered to eat posole, tamales, and sweet empanaditas, but he had not been hungry and was unable to join in the merriment celebrating Christ's birthdate. Later the vatos came by and dragged him to a party at Old Town, but drinking and getting high on mota didn't seem to be an answer either, so he had slipped out and walked home alone.

He stopped on the brown, frozen grass and remembered the autumn days he and Cristina had shared there. They had walked for hours across the yellow carpet of alamo leaves, and they had run and played like children, falling on the grass and covering themselves with golden leaves. The aroma of autumn had been as sweet as their love. Now a breeze stirred and he thought he smelled again the fragrance of her hair. He turned but there was no one there. He was alone in the wide, empty park. The trees around him were bare and the sky was overcast with the drabness of winter.

Once the trees had been as green as the infancy of their love and each day held an excitement that made them drunk with joy. He felt her presence as he had then. In his thoughts he slipped his arms around her waist and held her close; he tasted the sweetness of her lips. Time had stood still in the light of her soft, brown eyes and there was no beginning nor end to the days they spent together, nor to the moments that captured their love. They swore their love was for eternity. Now, that excitement of the late summer and the fall had passed into cold, dark winter.

He thought he heard her call his name and his pulse quickened and he turned, expecting to see her come running across the park into his arms. She was not there. And still the perfume of her body and her flowing hair lingered everywhere and to break the haunting, painful memory he ran across the park and filled his lungs with air until they hurt, and the stabbing pain helped to erase the thoughts that tumbled through his mind.

Cristina also felt the pain of their parting, perhaps more poignant because it was her mother's command that enforced the separation. She stood by the kitchen window and hoped that Jason would come running across the Williams Street Exit as he had so many times before. She yearned for him to come and sweep her off her feet and hold her until she was filled with his love again. Without him her life had little meaning. She went about the house doing her work mechanically, and when she looked out the window and saw only the dull gray of the yards tears filled her eyes. At night she played their favorite song over and over until the pain brought tears and she could cry herself to sleep.

The small gift she had bought him remained unopened under the faded Christmas tree. She had gone to a dance at the church, but she couldn't stay. She often walked alone and remembered all the places they had shared. Sometimes she thought of his betrayal and she wished that she could hate him and forget him, but her love went too deep and the confusion only increased her torment. With this disappointment weighing heavy on her heart she walked along the street on the last day of the year. She had just turned homeward when she ran into Sapo.

"Hey, what's up, baby! Long time no see——" he smiled, and as usual, he was high on dope.

"Lawrence——" she nodded and tried to pass him by. She didn't feel like talking to anyone, much less Sapo. Jason had told her about the fight at the park.

"Hey, hey, what's your hurry, ésa? No time to say hello to old friends? Getting too good for the fellows from this barrio? " he grinned sarcastically.

"No . . . I'm in a hurry, it's late." She was afraid of him. Everyone had tried to make him feel welcome when he returned from the reformatory, but he had gone back into shooting heroin immediately and so the girls in the barrio stayed away from him because when he was high he was crazy.

"Hurrying home to momma, huh, well that's good . . . Yeah, I like your jefita, she's all right! I like what she did to that pirujo boyfriend of yours! "

"Does that make you feel good, Sapo! " She jumped to Jason's defense.

"You damn right it makes me feel good, ésa! " Sapo's eyes narrowed. "I made a promise to get that vato, and sooner or later I will! I swore when I was in la reforma that nobody would ever touch me again, and they won't! Baby, I'll die before someone puts his hands on me again——" His mouth twisted with hate, spittle gathered at the sides. "In the meantime, I'm glad your jefita put him in his place. He ain't got no right comin' around here and messin' with our women! " He reached out and grabbed her wrist.

"I'm not your woman! " Cristina jerked away.

"Well, you're from this barrio, and you should stick to the vatos from this barrio! " He grinned and looked her over. "Like me——" he suggested.

"Like you? " Cristina winced, "you're sick, Lawrence——"

He reached out again, this time holding her close so she couldn't break away, he glared at her, "Yeah, well that's too bad, baby, 'cause it's all of you that makes me sick! "

"Even your carnales, even Flaco and Frankie——" Cristina cried and struggled to get loose.

"I ain't got no carnales! " Sapo laughed crazily, "I lost all my brothers a long time ago, ésa, I'm alone——"

"That's your problem! You have no friends! " Cristina shouted.

He flung her away from him and stepped back. "Okay! " He shouted, "So I'm sick! But they did it to me! This pinche place did it to me! The beatings, the rules, the law, the guards at la reforma—— They did it! And now——" He was breathing hard, his nostrils flaring and trembling with rage as he swore his revenge, "——I'm going' do it back! And I'm goin' start with your friend, Jason! "

"Why, Sapo, he never did anything to you——"

"He hit me! " Sapo shouted, "He hit me, and I swore nobody's ever goin' to hit me again——"

"He didn't mean to, Sapo, he was only protecting his brother! "

"No! No! " Sapo shook his head wildly, "I don't care for reasons! I'm gonna get him! "

"Leave him alone, Sapo, please leave him alone," she pleaded.

He laughed. "It's good to see you begging, baby," he cried triumphantly, "you think you're so high and mighty, and here you are begging! " He laughed crazily, bobbing up and down.

"I just don't want to see him hurt——" She said simply and started to walk away.

"Wait a minute, baby! " Sapo called, "I'll make a deal with you. I'll leave him alone if you go to the New Year's dance with me tonight. Dig? " He grinned. She shook her head.

" ¡Orale! ¡Orale! " He shouted and ran up to her. "Okay, baby, I'll make you a better deal. Listen, ésa, I know why your old lady broke you and Jason up, it's 'cause she thought he was the father of Cindy's baby, right? Well, what if I told you who the real father is, huh? "

"You know! " Cristina gasped.

"Yeah, I know," he said coolly, "and if you'll be my girl at the big dance tonight I'll tell you."

Cristina moaned. Suddenly she realized that she had doubted Jason; she had not believed in him completely and that had kept her from fighting for their love. Now it might be too late.

"It was Benjie! " Sapo blurted out.

"Benjie! " she cried and reached out and grabbed his arms.

"Yeah, Benjie. He told me. She went to him on purpose; she

was really jealous after Jason didn't pay any attention to her, so she went to Benjie to get even with Jason! "

Cristina's nails cut into his flesh. Now she loosened her grip and turned away. She felt sick. "And all the time Jason knew, he knew . . ."

"Yeah, he probably knew——" Sapo nodded and wiped the sweat from his forehead. "How can you hide something like that from your brother——"

"Oh my God——" Cristina cried, and to keep from falling into the whirlpool spinning around her she ran. Choking sobs gripped her throat and tears washed her face, and behind her she heard Sapo call, "Hey don't forget the dance tonight! "

CHAPTER NINETEEN

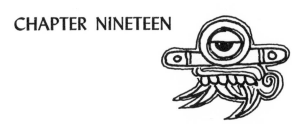

On the last day of December Willie kissed his mother goodbye, shook hands with his father, then waving goodbye to the barrio he went down to the Army recruiter and signed up. He bought a bottle of wine and got drunk with a couple of Indians from Santo Domingo while they waited for the bus. By the time Jason and Chelo got there he was drunk and sitting in the bus.

"Why did you do it, Willie? " Jason asked from the curb.

Willie leaned out the window and smiled. "I got tired of their silly games . . . I mean, I just can't go back and play their crazy act, that's not for me, anymore . . . Back there, everyone believes I'm crazy . . . What they don't know, is, they're crazy! Yeah. I figured it out . . . Here, wanna drink? " He held out the wine bottle.

"Nah, not now, Willie . . ."

"Well . . ." Willie winked and took a swig, "I don't want to be crazy like them. It's hell, 8 to 5, everybody be the same, stay quiet, keep in rows, screw it! I want to be me. Like your old man, Jason . . . he knows who he is, an' nothing can get to him . . ."

"Yeah, but why the Army? " Chelo asked and shivered. Gray, snow clouds were gathering over the volcanos.

"Why not? " Willie shrugged. "The place don't make any difference. Fort Bliss can be heaven or hell . . . so can Barelas . . . so can the fancy homes of the Country Club rich . . ."

"What about the strike, Willie . . . You kept saying the workers would win, and now you won't be here to see the end . . ."

"Yeah, I hate to run out," Willie nodded. "I'll leave this one to you two . . . and I'll be ready for the next one! " He smiled.

So there was really nothing to say, Willie had decided, and all they could do was joke about it. That helped to ease the vacuum he left.

"Well, they always said you were great Army material, Willie, you don't think! "

Willie laughed. "Yeah, by the time the rest of you chicanos get there I'll be a general. I'm so far ahead of the system they can't keep track of me anymore. I fought it, I resisted it, and I learned how it works, but now it's not interesting anymore. What's interesting is me, how I work, who I am, y toda esa chingadera——"

The bus driver called "All aboard! " and the bus jerked forward. Willie wiped his nose and waved goodbye.

"Hasta luego, Willie! " They waved from the curb and watched the bus disappear into the gathering gray mist of the storm.

"It's gonna snow tonight——" Jason shivered.

"Yeah. Damn, I can't believe Willie would do a thing like that! Remember the time he——" And Chelo went into one of Willie's crazy adventures, but Jason wasn't listening. He was thinking about what Willie had said, that he had to find himself, and he was thinking about the journey each one of them took to encounter himself. Willie wasn't crazy, he knew what he had to look for, which was more than most of them knew.

"——Ah, let's get the hell outta here! " Jason interrupted. They walked across the wet street, got in the car and drove back to the barrio.

"What do you want to do tonight? " Chelo asked.

"I don't know," Jason replied. He was thinking and the thoughts depressed him. Cristina was always on his mind; he worried about the mess Benjie was getting into with the barrio dope traffic; the barrio was sitting on a bomb, his father could light that fuse if he so chose, and now Willie was suddenly gone. My God, he thought, it seems like an eternity since I first came to Barelas.

"Have you seen Cristina? " Chelo asked.

"No," Jason answered, "her old lady won't let her see me . . . It seems like forever since that night at the church . . . I was just thinking, we've been through a lot since the summer, and a lot of things have changed, I mean we've all changed . . . Willie's gone, Pato's dropped out of school and is talking about getting married, the cuates are doing time for that crazy break-in they did . . . Henry, the strike, Cristina, everything. It seems like a lifetime."

"Yeah," Chelo agreed. He understood how Jason felt about

184

Cristina, and Willie had been a close friend. Jason was the only one who ever got really close to the family; he seemed to understand their insanity. "Maybe the best thing's to split, like Willie . . ."

"I don't think he ran away," Jason said, "the family just needed the money. His old man's been sick, and there's almost a dozen kids to feed . . . The responsibility fell on Willie . . ."

They drove in silence awhile then Chelo suggested they celebrate New Year's eve by going to the dance at the Center. "We can get the gang together tonight, and we'll get drunk, for Willie! "

"Orale," Jason agreed. "Beats staying home——" He secretly hoped Cristina would be at the dance. If she was he was going to explain everything to her and put an end to the stupid mess.

"Can you use Roberto's car tonight? "

"Yeah," Jason answered, "I'll ask him."

"Pick us up at the Red Ball——" Chelo called as Jason dropped him off. He drove home feeling better about the resolution he had made not to let anyone stand between him and Cristina. It was strange how quickly the depression melted away once he made the choice. In different form, it was the same choice Willie had to make; and although it seemed more complex and of more consequence, it was the same choice his father would have to make. To act or not to act. It was that simple. The circumstances of each decision were different, but the common element, the decision to rule their lives, was the bond that united them.

He parked in the backyard then slipped into the kitchen and greeted his mother. She was busy preparing supper.

"Jasón," she greeted him warmly, "I'm glad you're home. The sala is full of men and I have no meat to feed them. Run to the store and get a pound of hamburger meat, for the chile——" She counted small change from her bowl in the cupboard and handed it to him.

He didn't argue but slipped back into the milky darkness and raced to Bromo's on Fourth Street; it was closed. He would have to go to el Super's, who never closed. There were no customers in the dingy supermarket. El Super and his wife looked surprised when they saw him.

"A pound of hamburger! " Jason ordered quickly. He cursed himself for coming, but he knew his mother would be disappointed if she could not flavor her chile with some meat, however meager it was.

El Super grunted and scratched his belly. "So, one of the Chávez boys, eh? I hadn't seen one of the Chávez troublemakers in a long time," he said to his wife. Then he turned to Jason and sneered, "You got the money, Chávez? " Jason threw the change on the table. "Bah, I should have a rule against people like you, but a cash sale is a cash sale——" He picked up a handful of red meat and threw it on the scale. "I hear your father's back to his old game, stirring the people up, making trouble——"

"He's not making trouble! " Jason answered through gritted teeth.

"——Yeah, they say he's speaking in tongues, shouting prophecies, well you know what I think? I think he's touched in the head, yeah, a crazy man and a blind man leading the masses! " He laughed aloud and his wife nodded her approval. "Well, it'll be all over when his trial comes up . . . They're going to lock him up and throw the key away, then we'll have some peace and quiet around here, um-huh . . . I tell you, the people don't want a revolution . . . no, all they want is peace and quiet, time to take things slow . . . it's good for business——"

"Is that why you tried to bribe him! " Jason burst out. He couldn't contain his anger any longer. He cursed himself again for coming, better to have gone without the meat.

"A lie! " El Super shot back. "There was no bribe! We merely tried to make see some reason, that's all——" he sputtered. "We gave him a chance to forget all this nonsense, to leave the barrio and go back where he came from . . . We tried to make him see that the people around here don't want any trouble! Oh sure, there's a few hotheads like Lalo and his gang, but for the most part people just want things to stay as they are . . . Yes, we have a good life here when things are quiet, the women raise their families and go to church . . . the men work when they want to, and some Saturdays there's even enough extra money for a few drinks. What more could people want, huh? Now he comes around, stirring them up, promising things he can't deliver——"

"My father never promised anything," Jason argued, "he only gives the people hope! "

"Hope! " El Super laughed. "So it is hope he gives them, huh. Well let me tell you something, my little pendejito, the people

186

cannot eat hope! That's right, they can't make a nice gravy out of hope, not like they can with the meat I sell! No, and they can't spice it with chile and wrap it up in a tortilla to eat! So, I ask you, of what use is this hope he gives them, huh? It's useless and therefore the people don't want it. No, what they want are beans and tortillas in their stomachs, a fat woman to lie with, and a little beer for Saturday night, that's all! And I should know, I've been selling them these things all my life! Is your father so stupid he cannot see that, huh? "

"But, papá," his daughter spoke up, "our people are not so heartless——"

"Cállate! " He reprimanded her for daring to speak up. "I know what I say! The people say Chávez saw a vision, well, of what use are visions to poor people, huh? What they wanted him to bring down from that mountain is something they could see and smell and touch, something they could eat or sell, instead he brings them visions and wild stories about the heart of a land that only the Indians know! Well, let me tell you, the heart of a people is here! " He slapped his huge stomach.

"There are many eyes and ears in the barrio! " His wife hissed, "Say no more to this little monkey! "

"Why not, vieja," el Super laughed, "there is nothing he can do. Those eyes and ears point fingers I can buy——" He turned to Jason. "Learn something while you can, muchacho, as long as people are hungry they can be bought. That is true, when it comes to survival men give up all these wild ideas about brotherhood and honor and justice. You make men hungry and you make them compete for a crumb of bread and each one will be as vicious as the dogs who fight for scraps in the alley. Yes, man is selfish, he'll take care of himself first, he will never have the strength that unity creates because of his personal envidia—— Uh-huh, and when their luck turns against them and they have to choose between their personal survival or the brotherhood of their raza, well then, I'll bet you all the money in the world that they'll leave your father to rot on his mountain——"

He tossed the package of meat at Jason, and Jason caught it and ran. Outside, he stood on the sidewalk, trembling with frustration and rage. He had wanted to answer el Super, but he had not found the words, and inside he felt sick because he knew that he had

187

often wondered about the very things the man had said.

The dogs that lived in the alley behind the store whimpered around him. They were the shadows of hunger in the night, they were the shadows of poverty that hung over the barrio. They had smelled meat and they had closed in, but tonight they would not have to fight for it, because to find release from the impotence he felt Jason tore open the package and threw it in their midst. The pack of dogs fell on it, snarling and ripping at it, swallowing without chewing the raw pieces of meat. Then with bared fangs they turned on each other and fought for the last, dirt-covered scrap. Jason watched them, and he thought about what el Super had said, then he cursed because he thought el Super had beaten him. He turned and ran home. He was out of breath when he burst through the door.

"¡Mijo! " His mother cried, "¿Qué pasa? What is wrong? "

"Nothing," Jason shook his head, "I ran——"

"And the meat? " She asked.

"The store was already closed, mamá, I am sorry." He lied so that he wouldn't have to explain.

"No need to be," she smiled and reached out and ran her fingers through his dark, curly hair. "The meat was only to please our guests, there is plenty of food. I have a pot of beans I cooked today, chile de riztra, arroz guisado con jamón, natillas, and I'm finishing the tortillas—— a feast for poor people. Go and greet the neighbors," she nodded.

He walked into the living room and stood by the door. His father was speaking and he did not want to interrupt.

"——I thought I understood my earth," Clemente was saying to the gathered company, "after all, I am a man whose flesh and bones were molded by the earth of the llano, its weathers and moods are part of my spirit, but when I walked on that mountain I felt a power I have never felt before . . . and it was only when I reached out and grabbed hold of the people in the river that I could feel the heart of the land . . ."

"¡Santo Niño de Atocha! " old Manuel's wife crossed herself.

"I held a fiery sword," Clemente nodded and his eyes glowed with the secret of his vision, "and with that sword I cut down the snakes of steel that suck the blood of our people and poison their will! "

"It is the sword of the Lord," Primo's wife nodded, "it is a sign sent to you, Clemente . . . God has touched you."

"Perhaps," Clemente smiled, "but I think that in daring to touch the manswarm in the river I touched Him . . ."

They were silent for awhile, imbued in the beauty of Clemente's story, overcome by the symbols that spoke to their hearts. Then Primo stood up and shook his head.

"Yes, a beautiful story . . . but there are too many signs in it, too many things to explain. I still don't know if the mountain is out there somewhere . . . or if it's all in one's head? " He looked at Crispín for an answer.

Crispín shrugged. "Which would be the most difficult mountain to climb? " he asked simply. "And wouldn't a man rather bathe in a natural river than in the river of his humanity? "

"Yes," Manuel pondered aloud, "this humanity which Clemente has touched, they can be ugly and cruel creatures at times . . ."

"Ah," Primo complained, "let's have a drink of wine before you get me drunk on words! " They laughed and joined him, and the talk turned to the more practical matters of the upcoming trial and the tension which had resumed after the short Christmas break.

CHAPTER TWENTY

After supper Jason went to Roberto's to borrow the car. For awhile he played with the baby and listened as Roberto and his friends discussed the strike. Roberto had become his father's right hand man, and during the time Clemente had been sick Roberto had kept the men organized and at the picket lines. He didn't completely understand his father's vision, but he was good at working directly with people and after he lost his job with the city he helped organize the workers into a tightly knit group which kept growing in numbers and strength. A fervor which had been missing before now was felt as the young workers talked about their destiny.

"¡Huelga! " became their byword and the sense of pride it carried infiltrated the barrio and spread throughout the city.

"Equal rights to the workers! " they shouted and held up clenched fists, and a religious urgency sounded in their words. People everywhere were hearing about the strike at the barrio and messages of support began to come in.

"We'll stay on strike until we accomplish our goals! " one of Roberto's friends shouted earnestly, and his excitement mingled with apprehension because he knew the struggle would be long and it involved a deep commitment to the forging of a destiny. Still, the times excited them, as all people feel excitement when hope stirs in the wind.

"Now let's get to work! " They settled down and began to go over the list of names of men who had not yet joined their cause. They discussed possible ways to approach these workers they still called brothers, although aside they joked there were a lot of blind brothers around.

Jason kissed the baby and quietly said goodbye to Rita. He slipped into the cold night, wondering about those who had not yet found their place in the movement. There were many who continued in their well-worn ruts, refusing to see the clouds of the gathering storm, unable to sense the time of recreation which surrounded them. Sometimes Roberto talked about the men he tried to enlist in the cause and he said he felt sorry for them because they could not make their commitment and so lived out their existence in the limbo of indecision. Well, sooner or later they all had to decide how to live, and in a few years he and the rest of the vatos would have to take on what his father and the workers began here tonight.

He shivered as he slipped into the frozen car. The air was tense with ice; an eerie, yellow cast filled the barrio as the city lights reflected off the pale gray storm that hung over the city. Wisps of snow and ice froze on the car windows. He backed the car slowly out of the yard. For a moment he saw his mother framed against the kitchen window and he felt like going inside and asking her for her blessing, but he hesitated and the feeling passed. He drove to the Red Ball and picked up the vatos.

They were glad to see him. They knew they were drifting apart, so the reunion made them feel good. They bought some beer and drank as they cruised up and down Central. Pato lit a couple of Barelas queens, two well-made marijuana cigarettes, so they rode high on the smoke, bien locos. They passed the communal cigarette, took deep tokes, drank beer and got high. They told old stories about old times, and they laughed.

"Too bad old Willie's not here——"

"Yeah. We're all here, except Willie."

"I'm going to get drunk tonight, bien pedo! For Willie! " Dickie shouted.

" ¡Orale! For Willie! " They roared with laughter and raised their beers and drank.

"How's married life, Pato? " Pete asked. Pato wasn't married yet, but they teased him because his girl had him by the horns.

"Don't worry about me," Pato laughed, "I'm getting plenty. It's you guys at school I worry about——"

"We're doing fine," Dickie assured him, "we got this new English teacher at school that is built like God had a lot of time on His hands when he put her together. Man, is she nice! " He smacked his lips.

191

"She's not married and she's friendly to us big boys," Pete smiled, "the only trouble is she spends all her time in the teachers' lounge, smoking, drinking coffee, and flirting with that queer who teaches history, what's his name? "

"Hey, truchas," Pato warned them, "la ley! " A squad car passed them by.

"Man, they're really crusing Barelas——"

"It's because of the strike, they're afraid. Lalo and his boys have enough stuff put aside to make a small war——"

"Ah, they breathed down our backs long before the strike! " Pato cursed. "They should go cruise up in the Heights for awhile, and leave us alone! "

"Man, they don't bother up there because there's no marijuana or chiva up there——"

"Like hell there ain't, ése! Those gabachos up there are pushing more junk than all the tecatos in the valley put together! Look at it this way," Pato intoned, "you gotta have money to finance the stuff, and that's where the money is. Hell man, the only reason the pushers get busted in the barrio is because that's where the blue-eyed boys are looking for them, but let me tell you something, one of these days they're going to look in their own back yards and they're going to find a mess, a big mess——"

They had finished the beer and the last tokes on the roaches. As they drove by the dark and deserted Roosevelt Park they threw out the empty bottles, like they had done so often in the summer, much to the chagrin of summer lovers. Now the park was bare and empty, and the boys of summer could only laugh if one of their bottles exploded agaisnt one of the giant elm trees.

"Damn, there used to be some good rumbles here at the park," Pato reminisced.

"Yeah, in the good old days," Dickie agreed.

The Center was packed when they arrived. They worked their way past a madding crowd of gyrating be-boppers who danced crazily to Fats Domino, Little Richard, Bill Haley and the rest. The loud music made them feel cool, and as high as they were they felt they owned the world. The crowd parted to let them by and they joked with everyone, learning that the biggest thing in store for the night was a rumble that was going to take place between Albuquerque High and St. Marys. The Christmas basketball tournament had created bad feelings, so everyone was just hanging around waiting for the jocks to show up and start the fight. But that was nothing new to los vatos whose life revolved around rumbles.

"The hell with that kid stuff! " Pato growled, "I'm going to dance while I'm here——" He wandered off, always looking for the easy piece.

Dickie and Pete paused to talk basketball with some of the other vatos they knew from school, so by the time Jason and Chelo stumbled into fat Gloria they were alone. The high school crowd was thick and tightly packed and it was very dark on the dance floor, so Jason didn't recognize her until she spoke.

"——Did you know that Cristina's here? " she shouted, holding her sweating face close to his and breathing bubble-gum breath at him. Jason shrugged. He figured she would be here, in fact it was the only reason he had come. He had resolved to talk to her that night, if need be to explain everything to her, but either way he wasn't going to continue to let other people run his life. But he wasn't prepared for the other thing big Gloria shouted at him above the dinning blast of music.

"She's with Sapo! "

"Sapo? " Jason asked. He shook his head. She had to be kidding.

"No," Gloria wiped the edges of her mouth and shook her head, "it's true! I don't know what's going on either, but she looks scared——" And she pointed off to the corner.

Jason turned and caught sight of Cristina. Whatever was happening wasn't right, so he was going to straighten it out. He worked his way across the dance floor, skirting the wild dancers at first then pushing them aside as his worry mounted. The feeling of limbo he had lived with for weeks melted away as he rushed towards her, but it seemed that the more he fought the dancing crowd the thicker it became and the more it resisted. Finally her name burst from his lips, and he reached out and touched her hand. She only had time to turn and stretch her hand towards him before Sapo leaped between them.

"Jason——" She cried.

"Stay back! " Sapo shouted. He reached out and grabbed Jason's outstretched arm. Jason pulled and sent him sprawling into the dancers. A girl screamed. Someone shouted, "Blows! Ruuuuum-ble! "

"Cristina——" Jason pushed aside the excited crowd to grab her, but the gangs from the two high schools were already flooding across the floor, sweeping him back. Small fights broke out everywhere, girls screamed and ran, and at the same time someone threw a switch and the lights went out. Jason felt someone hit him, but whoever it was didn't have time to land a second blow. Chelo's right hook exploded and sent the vato down.

"Did you see Cristina? " Jason shouted above the roar.

"Sapo grabbed her! " Chelo pointed towards the door. They pushed their way free of the raging melee and ran into the parking lot in time to see Sapo's car dragging out.

"Let's go! " Jason shouted. He gunned the car out of the lot, spinning and squealing ahead of a trail of flying gravel and the smell of burning rubber.

"Where do we go? " Chelo asked. They had lost sight of Sapo's car. They peered down the empty street through a frozen windshield. "——Sapo can hide anywhere in Williams or Sanjo," he cursed.

"We'll start there! " Jason nodded. He opened up the car down the one-way, made a squealing turn onto Broadway then turned at La Paloma Bar and searched the streets of Williams. The barrio was quiet, the frozen streets deserted.

"How about Cristina's house? " Chelo suggested.

"It's worth a try," Jason agreed. He stopped in front of her house and ran to the door. Cristina's mother appeared at the kitchen door.

"You——" She gasped. "I told you never to come here again! " She was going to slam the door but he blocked it.

"I know, Mrs. Sánchez, but it's important! Jaspon pleaded. "Is Cristina here? "

"No," she shook her head hesitatingly, "she's at the dance, at the Center——"

"She was with Sapo," Jason nodded.

"With Sapo? Of course not," she frowned, "she went with the girls—— Why would she be with Sapo? Has there been an accident? " she asked. There was something in Jason's sense of urgency that made her knit her brow and cry out the Virgin's name.

"No, nothing to worry about," Jason answered, but he knew something was very wrong. Cristina had lied to her mother to go to the dance with Sapo, and he didn't know why.

"There is something wrong! " Cristina's mother cried and clutched at him. "If she's with Sapo . . . but no, she couldn't be, she went with Gloria . . ."

"I have to go! " Jason said and pulled away. "That boy's crazy, Jason! " he heard her shout as he ran towards the car, "Bring her back! Find her and bring her back! "

"Anything? " Chelo asked.

"She hasn't been here," Jason answered and started the car.

"Damn! " Chelo swore. He knew the barrio was too big to search. Sapo could hide in a million places, and as crazy as he was there was no telling what he'd do.

"Flaco and Frankie might know——" Jason thought aloud.

"Hey! " Chico snapped his fingers, "They were at the Red Ball when we left! They were waiting for Benjie! "

"Let's go! " Jason cried. He swung the car around and thundered across the Williams Street Exit, then he turned up Fourth Street and gunned it towards the cafe. There was a crowd gathering at the door of the small cafe as they pulled up.

"Looks like trouble," Chelo muttered.

They jumped out and pushed past the onlookers. In the cafe a few men were gathered around a figure on the floor. The biting smell of gunpowder filled the room. Each man was shouting instructions, but in the excitement nothing was getting done for the bleeding man. Conio was shouting into the telephone that he wanted an ambulance, while his wife knelt at the small altar of the Virgin at the counter.

Jason grabbed the groaning figure and turned him over. It was Frankie. He moaned and clutched at his stomach where a gaping hole spurted blood. "Hijo'ela chingada . . . I'm dying . . ." he cried when he saw Jason. The blood soaked his coat and shirt and formed a pool around him. He coughed and spit up blood, and Jason knelt at his side and lifted his head so he wouldn't choke.

"¿Qué pasó? "

"Sapo," Frankie answered weakly, "he shot me . . . We were sitting here . . . just talking, ése, waiting . . . and he came in, crazy as hell, and he was gonna kill Benjie——" The pain that was burning

195

his insides was also threatening his life and he clutched desperately at Jason's arm. "Damn, I don't want to die! " he cried.

"It's okay," Jason tried to calm him, but he could see the blood was draining away and there was nothing he could do. He looked hopelessly around him, but there was nothing any of the men could do.

"Better call a priest," one said and shrugged. They could see that the blood which had come in spurts was now a dribble, and Frankie was pale.

"The ambulance's coming . . ." Conio said from the phone, and they heard the wail of a distant siren.

"And listen! " his wife whispered. They listened and thought they heard the sound of the blue guitar. "Crispín's coming! "

"Yeah," Jason reassured Frankie, "he'll know what to do! Hang on."

"Orale . . . órale," Frankie mumbled. He kept talking to himself because it was the only way he could keep away the shadow that was stalking the room and threatening to engulf him. "——I tried to talk to him . . . but he was crazy . . . He aimed at Benjie, and I laughed . . . Hey, we're friends . . . I laughed . . . and then he shot me. I fell, and he ran out, with Benjie . . . and the girl . . ."

"Cristina! " Jason looked at Chelo. "He's got Cristina and Benjie! "

"Where? " Chelo shouted, but Frankie's eyes had closed.

Death was like a shadow that moved from behind the sun to close his eyes. Death was the son of the empty dark night, and he sucked the blood dry for his chingada madre, and he smiled as he gazed upon her dark womb . . . la Llorona was his sister, who cried at being robbed . . . but just before the wind could moan with a new soul the angry music of the blue guitar shattered the grasp of darkness!

"Crispín! " Jason shouted. The old man broke through the crowd. Other men followed him, but he was the first to arrive. He reached into the wound and grabbed the torn artery and clamped it shut. And the music that had thundered around them and the wailing of the siren grew still.

"Will he live? " Jason asked. Crispín nodded. "I have to know where he took Benjie and Cristina! " Crispín rubbed Frankie's forehead and his eyes fluttered open.

196

"Where did he take them! " Jason shouted in his face.

"The water tank——" Frankie gasped and passed out again.

"Go quickly! " Crispín nodded, "I will stay with him . . ." Manuel and the other men had arrived, and two ambulance attendants were already rushing through the door with their stretcher in hand. Jason pushed through the crowd and bolted towards the car.

"The water tank at the shops! " he shouted to Chelo who was on his heels.

They jumped into the car and turned back towards the tracks. At the railroad crossing Jason swung the car sharply to the left and entered the dark maze of buildings and boxcars. The bouncing headlights stabbed through the darkness as he gunned the car between the tracks towards the black outline of the water tank. The cold front of the storm suddenly howled around them and buffeted the car. The lights of the car cut an insignificant path in the darkness of the canyon that towered over them. Just when they thought the tracks would narrow down and engulf them they parted and in the clearing ahead stood the round, massive hulk of steel. The round tower rose into the cold, milky sky, thrusting its impotent power into the icy sky of the barrio. Even in the dark of night the faded letters stamped on the side of the black monarch picked up enough light to be seen. SANTA FE. The Holy Faith, embedded in a faded cross, a perverted faith in steel.

"There! " Chelo shouted and pointed at Sapo's car. The lights flashed across the clearing and illuminated the darkness. Cristina stood by Sapo's car. Jason hit the brakes and bounded out of the car.

"Cristina! " He shouted above the deep, rumbling thunder of the shops.

"Jason——" She cried and ran into his arms. "Oh, my God——" she sobbed in relief, then she turned and pointed. "He made Benjie climb! He said he'd shoot me if Benjie didn't climb——"

Jason looked, and spotted Benjie. He was halfway up the tank, clinging to the cold, steel rungs of the ladder that ran to the top of the tank.

"Beeennnnn-jie! " Jason shouted into the driving wind, "Come down! " At that moment Sapo jumped from behind the car. He pointed the zip-gun at Jason.

"Noooo! " He shouted. He grinned savagely at Jason. "I knew

197

you'd come, now you can see your brother get it, 'squadro——" He pointed the pistol at Jason's forehead and shouted over his shoulder, "You climb, Benjie! You climb to the very top or I'll blow your brother's brains out! Just like I did Frankie! "

"Get back, Jason! " Benjie called, "He's crazy! He shot Frankie! " The wind whipped his words away as he clung precariously to the ladder. He pushed himself, but he couldn't climb anymore. The cold steel rungs of the ladder had burned his hands raw.

"He can't climb! " Cristina cried. "Let him down, Sapo! " she pleaded, "you've punished him enough! He's going to fall——"

"Climb! " Sapo shouted crazily.

Jason turned to face him. "No, Sapo, he's not going to climb anymore! Come down, Benjie! " he shouted over his shoulder and walked slowly towards Sapo. "Give me the gun, Sapo, it's all over . . . You've hurt enough people tonight . . ."

"No," Sapo shook his head and backed away. "I'm going to make him climb . . . I'm going to make him pay . . ." He felt Chelo circling behind him. They were drawing him into a trap and he had to act quickly, so he pointed the gun at Jason. "Nobody ever messes with el Sapo," he laughed, but he couldn't fire. There was something about Jason that reminded him of the young boy he had killed during the barrio riots. Suddenly his hand was trembling uncontrollably and he was pleading with them to stay back.

"Give me the gun, Sapo," Jason repeated.

"No! " he shouted and jumped back. "No, stay back! Don't touch me! Nobody touches Sapo! " In desperation he whirled and fired blindly at the figure on the tank.

The flash of fire was followed by a loud report that went echoing down the maze of boxcars. He had not aimed and so it was by chance the the bullet smashed into Benjie's left hand and shattered it. The mangled hand jerked away from the rung it had held so tenaciously. For a terrifying moment Benjie dangled by his right hand, but he couldn't hold on. His feet slipped on the frozen rung and he plummeted downward. There was a dull thud as he struck the frozen ground.

Jason leaped forward and jerked the pistol out of Sapo's hand, but it was too late, he had already done his damage. He cursed and raised the pistol to hit Sapo, ready to pack into one blow the rage and frustration he felt, but he couldn't strike the pitiful figure cringing before him. Sapo fell to his knees, covered his head and began to cry. Jason flung the pistol into the darkness and turned and ran towards his brother. Chelo and Cristina were already kneeling by him.

"Thank God, he's alive," she whispered. They eased him on his back and covered him with their jackets. Benjie groaned and opened his eyes.

"Chingao——" he moaned, "what in the hell happened? You okay, Cristina? " he mumbled.

"I'm okay——" she nodded.

"I'm sorry I didn't come in time, Benjie," Jason shrugged. He blamed himself for what had happened.

"Hey," Benjie smiled weakly, "you came in plenty of time, brother. I'm alive, ain't I? I'd ah never made it to the top. Besides, I'm not feeling any pain, not even where the bullet hit my hand——" He tried to raise his hand to show them where the bullet had hit, but he couldn't. At first he thought his arm was broken, but when he tried again and didn't feel any pain his bewilderment changed to shock. "I can't move my arm! " He cried, "Damn, I can't move my arm——" He tried to lift his right arm, but he couldn't move that either, then he tried to turn to get up but he remained motionless. He exerted all the effort he could muster, but nothing happened. Fear swept over him and he cried as loud as he could into the stormy night, "Oh, my God! I can't move! I can't move! "

"Take it easy, Benjie," Jason tried to comfort him, "you'll be okay——" He looked helplessly at Chelo and Cristina and they shook their heads. They didn't understand what had happened either, except that he was paralyzed, that his back was broken and he was crying and shivering. They tried to comfort him.

"Yeah, it's going to be okay," Chelo said hoarsely, "help is coming——" He nodded in the direction of the stabs of flashlights that cut the darkness. Men's voices called, and a siren sounded at the Williams Street crossing.

"You'll be okay," Cristina whispered through watering eyes. She caressed his forehead, then took his wounded hand and laid it tenderly on her lap so the grime and dirt of the shops would not contaminate it. "You'll be all right," she nodded and wiped the tears flowing from his eyes.

They were all crying when Roberto found them, silent tears watered their eyes and cheeks because they were tired and cold and hurt by the harsh reality and the pain they shared.

CHAPTER TWENTY-ONE

And where was the golden deer of the ancient legends? Did he sleep in the lands south of Aztlán, unaware of the sufferings of his people? Would his sister, the new moon of the new year, rise without him?

The golden deer stood still. He pawed the fresh earth of eternity, sniffed the fathomless space of his journey, then he leaped northward into a trail of blazing glory that would take him to his people . . .

The Sandía Mountains wore a thin band of snow along the crest, and in the pine forests the deer moved restlessly to lower elevations, seeking the protection of the deep canyons. The new moon moved gently over the mountain and looked down on the people of Barelas. And because it was the new moon of the new year it wore two faces, one looking into the past from whence it had risen, and the new face looking forward into the future and the cycles it would complete as the people struggled toward their destiny. The moon smiled, because the returning sun smiled, but still the storm hung over the land like a cold, gray sheet and did not allow the sun to shine through.

More snow threatened. There was no color to the sky this day.

The men of Barelas gathered in old Manuel's yard to talk; they stamped their feet and pressed close to the fire Manuel kept burning in the half-barrel. They extended their arms to catch the warmth of the fire and they rubbed their hands together to spread the heat. From time to time one of them would turn to warm his back, then he could not help seeing Clemente's home across the street. The small, adobe home made him feel uneasy, because each one already knew what had happened the night before.

Now, three men from South Barelas came up the frozen, snow-covered street. The men watched in silence as the three men in flowing, Army-surplus coats approached the group. They nodded a terse greeting. The three men had come to hear Manuel's story. The group parted and allowed the strangers room at the warm fire. The three men shared a bottle of wine, which they now passed around so that each man could drink. Then without words they looked at Manuel and their haunting eyes commanded him to tell his story once more. The story had already spread throughout the barrio, but they had come to hear it from the lips of the man who had been there.

"I am an old man," Manuel shrugged, "a simple man. I have been a woodcutter all my life, but one learns about the life of man and woman over the years of delivering their wood. I have seen them at their best and at their worst, I have seen life and I have seen death—— and last night death was in Conio's cafe. I could smell death, I could feel his presence hovering over that boy, I thought for a moment I had seen him. He seemed to be wrestling with the music of life which seemed to surround Crispín, and I swear to you by God Almighty that I had never witnessed anything like that in my life——" He paused, as if the recalling of the scene made him tired. And it was true, delving into his soul to try to understand what he had seen exhausted him. It was the first time in over seventy years that he had not risen with the dawn, axe in hand, to ring in the sun at the woodpile. He shivered and felt tired and old, like the gnarled old piñon trees he brought down from the mountains to split.

"Then he has found the melody," one of the three strangers whispered.

"I do not know——" his friend shook his head.

"Go on," they begged Manuel.

"——Well, there was something like an explosion, a thunder without sound, a feeling, and the shadow of death was gone. I turned to Crispín and he was trembling and pale, as if the music I heard had gone through him, as if his soul was the melody—— He fell into my arms and I had to help him home. By that time the young doctor in the ambulance was already taking the boy to the hospital, where they will patch him up, and call it a miracle of their medicine——" He shook his head in wonder.

"Well, by the time I got home the other thing had happened; I did not know it yet, but somebody must have brought the news to Clemente. His boy had fallen off the water tank at the shops, his back was broken and he was paralyzed, barely alive—— Anyway, I saw him leave the house, he was alone and he was carrying his sledge hammer. I called to him, but he did not answer, he kept walking down the dark road towards the shops. I stood here for a few minutes, thinking and letting the cold clear my jumbled thoughts, and when I finally realized where he was going, I called Roberto at the hospital. He came and we drove to the shops and began looking for Clemente——"

The men listened intently. Those who had already heard the story knew that in Clemente's tragedy lay a part of the meaning of their own strengths and weaknesses.

Manuel shivered. "It was like searching a graveyard where the earth has spit up empty coffins—— Anyway, when we found the first splintered boxcar we knew why Clemente had brought his hammer; he was going to bring down that dark place which has caused so much suffering. The slashes and dents of his hammer were everywhere! Switches were broken, lights shattered, and even the boxcars showed signs of his wrath! We moved quickly down the line, and then we heard the ringing sound. Oh, what a hellish sound! It rang like the bells of hell in that cold blizzard! "

"What was it? " One of the three strangers asked.

"It was Clemente," Manuel continued, "standing at the foot of the water tank where his son had fallen, striking at the tank, trying to bring down that tower of the devil! Blow after blow rang in that cold night, but what could he do with a single hammer? He struck with all his might, and the blows merely glanced off that cold, hard steel——

"Some of the private guards the bosses have hired were already there when we arrived, but they made no move to arrest him or to interfere. And some of the workers of the graveyard shift came, and like us they could only stand and stare. I tell you my friends, we have created something we cannot destroy; we are slaves to the steel. Each man there understood that. Yes, we felt his rage, and we saw how insignificant a man has become, and so we pitied him, and as we pitied him we pitied ourselves. We could not move because we respected him, and because we were afraid.

"Finally, his sledge hammer splintered, it fell apart in his hands. Then he pounded the tank with his bare hands, until his fists were crushed and bloody, and exhausted he fell to the ground. Only then did Roberto approach him, carefully and with all the love a son has for his father he pulled him away from that place of so much pain. Oh, I felt a pity for that man as I have never felt before, and I am not ashamed to tell you that I cried. I cried for him, and I cried for all of us——" He paused and looked towards Clemente's home. It had been quiet all morning; the women were at the hospital keeping a vigil on the boy; Clemente had gone into shock and could not speak.

"——Such is the tragedy of our lives," old Manuel nodded.

The men were silent. As old Manuel told the story it became their own story, and the meaning became clearer as the story was retold. All day Manuel repeated the story, and still those that had heard it did not leave. The crowd grew, more fires were started. The women of the barrio brought food so that those who kept the vigil might eat. Even the pachucos joined the older men of the barrio, lending their youth and impatience to the waiting which was the silence before the storm. All of the strikers were there, and many of the people who had never supported the strike now came and joined the throng.

"He is resting now," an old man spoke and looked across the street.

"But he will speak soon," a woman added, "it is for that we wait. We have faith——"

"Bah! " Lalo spit in the fire, "What good is faith! The only thing those sonofabitches understand is power, and we have enough people here to burn the damned place down! "

"It looks like it will snow again," Primo spoke into the vacuum Lalo's words had left. He looked up at the colorless sky.

"The sky of Barelas has always been dark for our people! " Héctor snarled.

"No, not always," old Manuel reminded them, "the laughter of our children and our music have lighted up many a day, and the love in our familias has made the sky bright. Yes, we have lived under the shadow of injustice for a long time, but we have not allowed injustice and poverty to make our existence drab and meaningless. We must remember that in these hard times——"

"There is one sure way to make those skies brighter! " Lalo argued, "and that is with dynamite and fire! The time and place are tonight, we must act now! Vamos! " He called to the men

204

who followed him. It was time to arm themselves and distribute the dynamite.

In the house the women had just returned from the hospital. Rita, who had stayed to nurse Clemente, asked about Benjie.

"He will live," Juanita answered and dropped exhausted into a chair, "but he's paralyzed—— The doctor said it will be a long struggle . . . It's too early to tell . . ." She closed her eyes to keep from crying.

"He was sleeping quietly when we left him," Ana added. "¿Y papá? " She asked about her father.

"He's been sitting by the window all day," Rita whispered, "staring out at the people—— There's hundreds out there by now. They kept arriving all day, they've come from all the barrios of the city, they've gathered from everywhere."

"What do they want? " Ana bit her lip to keep from crying. "Don't they know he can't help them! Can't they see he's hurt! "

"He is their leader," Juanita tried to soothe her sister. "It is expected that a leader suffer for his people——" She turned to help Rita put the supper on the table, but at that moment Clemente stood up and faced them. Roberto saw him rise and turned to look at him from where he sat with his son on the sofa. At that same moment Jason and Cristina entered, returning from her mother's home. Even Crispín awoke from his troubled sleep in the big chair by the wall heater and turned his blind eyes to Clemente.

"Clemente," Adelita rose and went to his side, "what is it? Are you all right? "

"How is my son? How is Banjamín? " He asked.

"He is sick, now," Adelita answered him, "but he will return to us——"

Clemente sighed deeply. "——La familia has been torn apart and scattered before, but it will come together again——"

"Sí, por el amor de Dios," Adelita nodded and tears filled her eyes, "we will be complete again."

Clemente held her hands. He looked into her soft eyes and saw the pain and fatigue written in them, but he also caught a glimpse of her strong faith and of her love for all of them.

205

"——The people are waiting," he said hoarsely.

"Yes——"

"I must go to them," he smiled. "They are a part of my family. We are one family, and there are many things that must be done so that the family can grow and flourish—— It would be easier to remain in the warmth and comfort of my home, or perhaps to go when it is not so dark and cold, but I can wait no longer! They have waited in the cold and in hunger for a long, long time. Now is the time to act. Crispín! " He turned to his old friend. "Can that old guitar of yours imitate the sound of a drum? For a revolution the roll of a drum is needed! "

Crispín smiled and strummed the blue guitar. The cadence of the drum-beat called them to attention.

"I must go," he whispered and leaned and kissed his wife.

She hesitated a moment, then she threw his coat over his shoulders and reached for her own. "I will go with you," she said simply.

"It can be a long and dangerous walk from here to the shops," he reminded her.

Adelita shrugged. "Our women have a long history of marching beside their men," she smiled, "what's a long walk, and what's a little danger, if we're together——"

He nodded in agreement. They went out together and walked among the people. The crowd grew silent and waited for him to speak.

" ¡Vecinos! " He called to his neighbors, testing his voice and strength against the cold gusts of wind that swept up the street. "All of you know of the tragedy that has fallen on my house—— But tragedy is not new to our lives, and with your faith and support we will overcome it. Now, the greatest tragedy is the paralysis which injustice and oppression inflict on our people! Tyranny sucks our dreams and turns them into nightmares, it dries the hope we have for our children and their future! We have endured enough. Let it end tonight! "

" ¡Basta! " The people responded to his call. "Enough! " They cheered, and Clemente saw in their swaying movement the flowing river of his dream.

"He speaks the truth," the old men nodded and gave their blessing to the movement.

206

"No more waiting! " The young ones whispered to each other, "No more ten paciencia, mijo, no more bullshit que es la voluntad de Dios! We're on the move! " They cheered and linked arms together.

"Burn everything! Destroy everything!" Lalo shouted. "Let our bodies be the first stepping stones over which the rest of our people will march to victory! "

Someone took a piece of piñon burning at one of the small fires and held the torch aloft. Instantly many torches appeared and lighted the darkness. Lalo leaped forward and handed Clemente a torch. Clemente took the torch and held it up. A great roar went up from the crowd as they cheered the revolution which had come.

"Yes! We will burn away oppression and injustice! " Clemente shouted and quieted the people. "But not with this fire! " He tossed the torch back at the astonished Lalo. "The real fire from heaven is not the fire of violence, it is the fire of love! "

The people listened intently. He was going to point the way and they were ready to follow.

"——We know that violence breeds violence, and that this fire the wayward god stole from heaven is the same fire that melts the steel and forges the chains that enslave us! What that god should have stolen for us mortal men is the pure fire that gushes from the soul of our people, from the foundation of our history—— Only that fire can burn down the temple of the false gods! "

He paused, seeking the words that would communicate the fervent feeling and truth he felt in his soul.

"I could not bring down that devil's tower," he confessed, "a thousand men with hammers could not destroy the temples of steel. They have built them too well, my friends, they are masters of this technology that destroys us—— They took our blood and bones and brains, the very thing that made us men, and they made us build the giant that has enslaved us! Take a thousand of these torches and put them to the cold steel, and you cannot melt the giant down! "

Lalo glanced nervously at Héctor, then he stepped back. The silent crowd waited, nodding for Clemente to continue.

"There is a heat more intense than the fire of the torch! " Clemente cried cheerfully. "And it can be rekindled at a moment's

207

notice! Wherever discrimination and injustice and oppression rear their ugly heads the fire can be called upon to burn them away! Wherever there is an honest man, a poor man, an oppressed man, the fire smoulders in his heart, ready to ignite and light his path! It is the fire of love that burns in each man and woman and child; it is the fire of the soul of our people which must serve us now! "

He wanted to tell them that it was the power of this love that he had felt in the depths of the lake in the magic mountain, and that the river of humanity in his dreams had substance in the love that was reflected from each man and woman. He wanted to tell them that the people he had met in his journey were the same everywhere, that they cried and laughed the same, that they felt joy and sorrow as acutely as anyone, and that they shared in the same life-stream which was their destiny to carry to a completion. But the roar of the people drowned out his words. They understood what he was saying, and at that point the river swelled to its crescent and thundered with love.

They cried with laughter and joy. The simplest message made them shout like jubilant victors. They could never be beaten! Never! Not as long as a single man dared to look for his humanity in the corners of his heart. That infusion of spirit into flesh which generations of wise men had described throughout the ages was the simple bond of love that gave the river its strength to surge and roar and cut its new channel into the future.

"Lead us Clemente! " The chorus shouted.

" ¡Adelante! " The young people cried.

Clemente and Adelita stepped to the front of the torchlight procession that began to move up the street.

"Play us a song, Crispín! " Clemented called in joy.

"Play us a song of things as we will make them! " Adelita smiled in her faith.

Crispín strummed a tune of liberation on the blue guitar. The people began to move, marching to a new step, singing the songs of the revolution which would create their destiny. Around the perimeter of the shops armed guards fingered their rifles nervously. The dogs they held on leashes growled uneasily. They could smell fear, but they were not trained to deal with the burning force that came singing up the barrio street. In the dark, cold night the blaring sirens announced the mobilization of an-

other force at the barricades, but the people did not hesitate.
" ¡Adelante! " They shouted without fear.